Endorsements

"In the current debates on Justification, particularly the so-called 'New Perspectives(s) on Justification,' it is all too easy to become confused. Part of the problem is a lack of clarity as to what precisely was the *Old Perspective*. Turning to the Magisterial Reformers would therefore seem essential. Calvin's treatment of justification in the *Institutes* is magnificent and essential, and it is good to have it in this pocket book form for easy reference. John Allen's early nineteenth century Latin translation is smooth and crystal clear. Nate Pickowicz has served us well."

Derek W. H. Thomas, Senior Minister, First Presbyterian Church, Columbia SC; Chancellor's Professor, Reformed Theological Seminary; Teaching Fellow, Ligonier Ministries

"John Calvin's articulation of justification by faith in *The Institutes* is classic, but reading *The Institutes* is daunting to some, and thus this treasure on justification may be neglected. What a wonderful idea to publish Calvin's work on justification separately, which is more accessible and digestible, especially with the edits and annotations which accompany it. Readers who encounter Calvin for the first time will find his words to be strikingly contemporary, as they experience the 'lucid brevity' of his writing and as they are reminded about the gospel of grace in Jesus Christ."

Thomas R. Schreiner, James Buchanan Harrison Professor of New Testament Interpretation and associate dean of the school of theology, The Southern Baptist Theological Seminary

"A world-class theologian, a renowned teacher, an ecclesiastical statesman, and a valiant Reformer, John Calvin is seen by many as the greatest influence on the church since the first century. As a guardian of the truth, Calvin was a heroic defender of the Christian faith. This stalwart of the gospel was convinced he must resist the many enemies who would attack its purity. The doctrine of justification by faith alone was the preeminent doctrine Calvin espoused and defended. Use this work to refresh yourself in the truth of this biblical doctrine and its centrality in the life of the church."

    Steven J. Lawson, President, OnePassion Ministries, Dallas, TX; Teaching Fellow with Ligonier Ministries; Professor of Preaching and Dean of the Doctor of Ministry program at The Master's Seminary; Executive Editor for *Expositor* magazine

"We sometimes hear that the Reformation is 'over.' The Reformation in point of fact is not over. Challenges to scriptural soteriology proliferate in the current day, some within Protestantism, some outside out. Pastor-theologian Nate Pickowicz has done Christ's church a great service by collecting John Calvin's razor-sharp reflection on the biblical doctrine of justification. This is a heady but readable little book. All who dive in will profit greatly, and will come away ready to carry the Reformation torch in our day."

    Owen Strachan, Associate Professor of Christian Theology and Director of the Residency PhD Program, Midwestern Baptist Theological Seminary; author, *Always in God's Hands: Day by Day in the Company of Jonathan Edwards*

"Life is too short not to read the great writings of the history of the church. Life is also too short not to meditate on the doctrine of justification by faith alone in Christ alone. Nate Pickowicz has served us well by pulling these two things together with his republication of Calvin's teaching on justification from Calvin's *Institutes*. While some have improperly insisted that Luther focused on the doctrine of justification and Calvin focused on the doctrine of election, a cursory reading of Calvin's treatment in this work will dispel any such misrepresentation. This focused volume serves to prove that the doctrine of justification by faith alone held a central place in the theology of Calvin, as it should in our own."

Nick Batzig, founding pastor of New Covenant Presbyterian Church, Richmond Hill, GA; managing editor of Reformation21

"It has been said that Martin Luther was the spark that ignited the Protestant Reformation but it was John Calvin who fanned the flame. He was arguably the greatest exegete, theologian, and polemicist that the Reformation produced. His sundry skills are on full display in the present volume as he declares and defends what he considered to be "the principal hinge by which religion is supported"—namely, the doctrine of justification by grace alone through faith alone in Christ alone. Centuries have come and gone since Calvin's day, yet his exposition remains a sure guide for all who seek and savour Christ."

J. Stephen Yuille, Associate Professor of Biblical Spirituality, The Southern Baptist Theological Seminary, Louisville, KY

"Like Luther, the Geneva reformer considered justification 'the hinge on which true religion turns.' Many criticisms of the doctrine today rehash those that Calvin refuted here so carefully and convincingly. It's wonderful to have many of his defenses of justification in one place!"

Michael Horton, J. Gresham Machen Professor of Systematic Theology and Apologetics, Westminster Seminary California

"Justification by faith alone was the essential doctrine that inaugurated the sixteenth century Reformation. It was this vital non-negotiable of the church that drove the pulpit ministry and theological trajectory of John Calvin. Nate Pickowicz has done the church a great service by reigniting the fire that blazed within the heart of Calvin for this biblical truth. May God use this reissued work to unleash legions of Christians and launch a new Reformation in our own day."

Dustin W. Benge, Teaching Fellow, Reformanda Ministries

"After recently celebrating the Reformation's 500th year anniversary, one might think that Justification by Faith Alone would be considered an evangelical 'given.' Sadly, there are many inroads by which human (i.e. Sinfully tainted) righteousness infects this doctrine and in fact, subverts it if logically followed. Calvin needs to be re-read so that every Christian comes face to face with the fact that initial justification cannot be changed, and that Christ's righteousness is both mandatory and sufficient. I commend my friend Nate Pickowicz and his reissue of Calvin on Justification. He has let Calvin be Calvin and for that, I am thankful."

Mike Abendroth, Pastor, Bethlehem Bible Church, West Boylston, MA; Host of No Compromise Radio

Justification
By Faith

ABOUT THE EDITOR

Nate Pickowicz is the pastor of Harvest Bible Church in Gilmanton Iron Works, New Hampshire. He is the author of *Reviving New England: The Key to Revitalizing Post-Christian America* and *Why We're Protestant: An Introduction to the Five Solas of the Reformation*. Additionally, he writes for various blogs, and has edited several books. He and his wife, Jessica, have two children, Jack and Elizabeth.

Foreword by **MATTHEW BARRETT**

JUSTIFICATION BY FAITH

JOHN CALVIN

Edited by **NATE PICKOWICZ**
Translated by **JOHN ALLEN**

Justification by Faith

Copyright 2018 by Nate Pickowicz

All rights reserved. No part of this edition may be reproduced in any form without the written permission from the author.

Published by: H&E Publishing, Peterborough, Ontario, Canada

This volume contains excerpts from a work by John Calvin (1509–1564), which is in public domain: *Institutes of the Christian Religion*; translated by John Allen (1813).

First Edition, 2018

Paperback ISBN: 978-1-989174-10-4
ePub ISBN: 978-1-989174-12-8
Hardcover ISBN: 978-1-989174-17-3

Contents

Foreword.. XIII
    Matthew Barrett

Introduction... XIX
    Nate Pickowicz

Justification By Faith

1. Justification by Faith
The Name and Thing Defined............................... 1

2. A Consideration of the Divine Tribunal................ 41

3. Two Things Necessary to Be Observed
in Gratuitous Justification....................................... 55

4. The Commencement and Continual Progress
of Justification... 65

5. Boasting of the Merit Subversive of God's Glory
and of the Gift of Salvation.................................... 95

6. A Refutation of the Injurious Calumnies
of the Law and the Gospel..................................... 109

7. The Harmony Between the Promises of the Law
and Those of the Gospel.. 117

8. Justification from Works Not to Be Inferred
from the Promise of a Reward............................... 143

9. On Christian Liberty.. 163

Scripture Index... 187

Publisher's Note

In this edition, the punctuation and capitalization have been modernized, some archaic words have been updated, and a few other slight editorial changes made.

Acknowledgments

Thank you to Chance Faulkner for your encouragement and excitement in bringing this publication to life. Additionally, thank you to Mike Abendroth for impressing the importance of Calvin's work on justification, as well as R.C. Sproul Jr. for unknowingly inspiring the idea for the book. My sincere thanks to Dr. Matthew Barrett for writing the foreword.

To R.C. Sproul
for a lifetime of contending for *sola fide*

Foreword

Matthew Barrett

How can I, a sinner, be reconciled to a holy God? That question has occupied the greatest minds of the Christian church because it is a question that is central to Christianity itself. The Bible is a book that confronts humanity with terrible news: you have rebelled against your good and benevolent Creator and now and forever stand under his just condemnation. But the Bible is also a book that presents humanity with the good news: The Father has sent his Son to reconcile you with God. Your Creator has become your Redeemer.

How is this possible? It is only possible because the Son of God himself became incarnate to represent us. As the God-man, he lived in perfect obedience to God's law, something everyone since Adam has failed to do. Yet he not only fulfilled the law we failed to obey, he suffered the penalty of the law that we violated and transgressed. Laying his own life down at the cross in our place, Christ Jesus became a sacrifice, absorbing the wrath that should have been ours, the punishment that our sin deserved. In doing so, love and justice kissed. On the one hand, God's love was displayed in all its radiance. Who gives his own son over to death? Only one who is so full of love that he would make the ultimate sacrifice. On the other hand, such love was not at the expense of justice but wrapped in benevolent holiness. In vain would God have loved us if he compromised the purity and integrity of his divine character. So, he stepped down from the heavens to take the penalty upon himself, and in doing so was then able to remain just while justifying anyone who trusts in him.

How is one to receive this great work of salvation? By faith. Turning to one's one works is a fool's errand, an attempt to justify our sinful selves before the God of infinite and eternal holiness. The only hope is to turn to someone outside ourselves, someone who can provide us with the righteousness and forgiveness we cannot create for ourselves. Now we come to the pivotal moment in the Bible's own story, the great announcement to sinners who have heard the good news of Jesus Christ. It is through faith in Christ alone that one is declared right with God. Upon faith in Christ, the guilt for one's sins is forgiven—Christ has paid our debt in full. Yet that is but half the story. For the righteousness of Christ is imputed as well. Remember, he not only suffered the penalty we incurred for breaking the law, but he obeyed the law we failed to fulfill. What a great, marvelous exchange: Christ has taken our sin, we have received his righteousness. None of this is our own doing; it is by grace alone through faith alone in Christ alone. Therein is the doctrine of justification. We, sinners, have been declared right with God.

This good news is the treasure of the church and one would think the church would protect it at all costs. Unfortunately, that has not always been the case. In fact, not only was this good news about justification forgotten at times but it was exchanged for a different gospel, one that relied upon man's efforts, merits, and righteousness to be made right with God. How ironic: that which made the good news so good, namely, its announcement of *free* mercy and *unmerited* grace, was replaced by a message that called upon the individual to add his own contribution to the work of Jesus Christ. The church entered this dark night of its soul at the end of the fifteenth century.

But after darkness came light—*post tenebras lux*. The sixteenth century reformers returned to the scriptures only to find they could not reconcile what the biblical authors said with the church's teaching. Risking their own lives, the reformers not only translated the scriptures into the common language of the people so that Christians could see the good news of salvation in Christ for themselves, but the reformers entered pulpits to proclaim that justification is by grace alone (*sola gratia*) through faith alone (*sola fide*) in Christ alone (*solus Christus*). Those solas (*solae*) proved liberating, freeing the medieval Christian from the uncertainty of a justification that depended in part upon one's own merits.

Few reformers were so gifted at communicating the evangelical doctrine of justification as John Calvin. As a young reformer, Calvin was content to spend the rest of his life in an ivory tower writing works of theology. Yet when he serendipitously passed through Geneva, he was persuaded to stay and preach the scriptures to the church. What started as a pilgrim's detour turned into a ministry that would last for a lifetime. In time, Calvin not only preached sermons and wrote commentaries on books of the Bible, but he also provided the Genevans, and all of Europe, with an expansive theology of the Christian faith in his *Institutes of the Christian Religion*. With memorable prose, scriptural fidelity, and theological acumen, the *Institutes* shed light on the doctrine of justification where previously there had been dark ambiguity. With clarity in his left hand and precision in his right hand, Calvin helped the average churchgoer understand the beauty of justification. "We define justification as follows: the sinner, received into communion with Christ, is reconciled to God by his grace, while, cleansed by Christ's blood, he obtains forgiveness of sins, and clothed with Christ's righteousness as if it were his own, he stands confident before the heavenly judgment seat" (*Institutes* 3.17.8). In but one sentence, Calvin has summarized the driving force of the Reformation. Forgiven and clothed in the righteousness of Christ, the sinner no longer had to fear the fires of purgatory, question the certainty of salvation, or attempt to do his or her best to somehow merit grace and remission of sins. Righteousness is a gift, said Calvin, given to all those who simply trust in the righteousness of Jesus Christ.

The good news of justification by faith alone defined Calvin's ministry but it should define any church today who claims to be evangelical. For that reason alone, Calvin's work on justification deserves retrieving, lest we too fall back into darkness and drift away from the light of the biblical reformation. Thankfully, Nate Pickowicz has made Calvin's treatment on justification accessible. I would encourage every pastor to read it so that this doctrine informs his ministry from start to finish. But I would also recommend it to every churchgoer. Here is a book to be read and re-read throughout your Christian life, lest you forget just how amazing grace is or what warmth the robe of Christ's righteousness provides. *Tolle lege*—take up and read!

Foreword

Matthew Barrett
Associate Professor of Christian Theology, Midwestern Baptist Theological Seminary; Executive Editor, Credo Magazine

Introduction

Nate Pickowicz

The battle of the Protestant Reformation was waged over this primary question: *How does a sinful person get right with a just God?* At the heart of it, the Reformers contended that sinners are justified (declared righteous) by God through faith alone in Jesus Christ. This is known as *sola fide*—"faith alone." The longstanding belief of the Roman Catholic Church was that justification was attained through the gradual infusion of righteousness through ritual observances and practices. In fact, when challenged, Rome doubled-down and issued a series of canons and decrees anathematizing those who would maintain justification by faith alone.[1] However, in his defense of the

---

[1] On the topic of justification, the Council of Trent (1545–1563) issued 33 canons and 16 decrees. For example: Canon 9: "If any one saith, that by faith alone the impious is justified; in such wise as to mean, that nothing else is required to co-operate in order to the obtaining the grace of Justification, and that is not in any way necessary, that he be prepared and disposed by the movement of his own will; let him be anathema." Canon 12: "If any one saith, that justifying faith is nothing else but confidence in the divine mercy which remits sins for Christ's sake; or, that this confidence alone is that whereby be are justified; let him be anathema."

doctrine of justification by faith, the Apostle Paul pronounces his own curse on those who would teach a divergent gospel based on works (Gal. 1:8-9); and by their rejection of the biblical teaching, Rome placed themselves under Paul's anathema.

Today, however, questions still arise surrounding the nature of the doctrine of justification. The battle of the Reformation, it would seem, is far from over. But there are those who question the need for such staunch convictions. After five hundred years, are we simply stuck in a battle of anathemas? Are Protestants and Catholics just two siblings fighting over the same parent? Is the doctrinal skirmish nothing more than a religious feud akin to that of the Hatfields and the McCoys? Many would have us believe this. In evaluating the essence of the division, Iain Murray rightly notes the danger we are in when we suggest that "there is no *vital and essential* difference between Christianity and Roman Catholicism. The real issue... is about the way of salvation, and, if the gospel recovered at the Reformation is the truth, then love for the souls of men and women warrants a division now as it did then."[2] In short, the gospel is at stake!

John Calvin wrote that justification "is the principal hinge by which [the Christian] religion is supported." Further, in his debate with Cardinal Sadoleto, Calvin declared that *sola fide* was "the first and keenest subject of controversy between us." If this point be removed, he argued, "the glory of Christ is extinguished, religion is abolished, the church destroyed, and the hope of salvation utterly overthrown."[3] And so, before we

---

[2] Iain H. Murray, *Evangelicalism Divided: A Record of Crucial Change in the Years 1950 to 2000* (Edinburgh: Banner of Truth, 2000), 243.

[3] Quoted in Terry L. Johnson, *The Case for Traditional Protestantism: The Solas of the Reformation* (Edinburgh: Banner of Truth, 2004), 76.

Introduction

wade into our primary text, we would do well to make a few preliminary observations.

The Doctrine of Justification

The Reformers are often accused of inventing the doctrine of justification by faith alone. The claim is that, while interacting with early church fathers like Augustine, they reinterpreted and reimagined justification to fit their new movement. When reading their works, however, one thing becomes clear; the Reformers did not derive their understanding of justification primarily from reading the early church fathers, but from careful exposition of the Scriptures. However, in their doctrinal formulations, there are a few key characteristics of their understanding of justification.

Justification is a Forensic Term

At the outset, the meaning of the biblical term "justify" takes center stage (cf. Rom. 3:28; Gal. 2:16; etc.). Martin Luther admitted, "Augustine got nearer to the meaning of Paul than all the Schoolmen, but he did not reach Paul. In the beginning I devoured Augustine, but when the door into Paul swung open and I knew what justification by faith really was, then it was out with him."[4] In studying the term, he observed that Augustine understood the Latin word *iustificare* to mean "to make righteous" and thereby turning the sinner *into* a righteous person.

But Luther, as well as the subsequent Reformers, broke with the traditional view of the term, tracing it back to the Greek verb *dikaioō*, understanding it to mean "to declare righteous."

---

[4] Quoted in Timothy George, *Theology of the Reformers* (Nashville: B&H, 2013), 69.

This declaration functions in a *legal* or *forensic* sense. According to R.C. Sproul, "Indeed, it is the legal issue on which the sinner stands or falls: his status before the supreme tribunal of God."[5] This understanding is opposed to the notion that sinners are made righteous by the *infusion* of divine grace.

Writing in the seventeenth century, Francis Turretin argues that justification "is never taken for an infusion of righteousness, but as often as the Scriptures speak professedly about our justification, it always must be explained as a forensic term." His gives five reasons: (1) the passages which treat of justification admit no other than a forensic sense, (2) justification is opposed to condemnation, (3) the equivalent phrases by which our justification is described are judicial, (4) Paul never used the word to speak of an infusion of righteousness, and (5) unless this word is taken in a forensic sense, it would be confounded with sanctification.[6]

Justification is Distinct from Sanctification

One of the more common problems in approaching justification is the pervasive desire of some to conflate it with the doctrine of sanctification. James Buchanan astutely notes, "Justification, although inseparably connected with, is essentially different from, sanctification; and the former is not founded on the latter, as its procuring or meritorious cause." He further notes the errors of two opposing parties—

---

[5] R.C. Sproul, *Faith Alone: The Evangelical Doctrine of Justification* (Grand Rapids: Baker Books, 1995), 116.

[6] Francis Turretin, *Justification*, trans. George Musgrave Giger, ed. James T. Dennison Jr. (Phillipsburg: P&R, 2004), 4-5.

by Popish writers, who have held that to justify is to make righteous inherently, by the infusion of personal holiness; and by antinomian writers, who have spoken as if the righteousness of sanctification, as well as that of justification, were imputed, and not infused or inherent.[7]

While both doctrines are clearly presented in Scripture, they are never confused or muddled together. On the symbiotic connection between the two, Calvin notes:

> Christ therefore justifies no one whom he does not also sanctify. For these benefits are perpetually and indissolubly connected, so that whom he illuminates with his wisdom, them he redeems; whom he redeems, he justifies; whom he justifies, he sanctifies… Do you wish, then, to obtain righteousness in Christ? You must first possess Christ; but you cannot possess him without becoming a partaker in his sanctification; for he cannot be divided.[8]

Christ's Righteousness is Imputed to the Believer

Due to the inherent sinful depravity of humanity (Rom. 3:10–18, etc.), it fast becomes clear that sinners are in desperate need of a righteousness that will be accepted by God. However, no such righteousness exists in them. The Reformers realized that sinners were in need of a righteousness outside of themselves — an "alien" righteousness — if they were to be justified. Luther writes, "Sins remain in us, and God hates them very much. Because of them it is necessary for us to have the imputation of

---

[7] James Buchanan, *The Doctrine of Justification* (1867; reprint, Edinburgh: Banner of Truth, 1961), 246.

[8] This volume, ch. 6, i.

righteousness, which comes to us on account of Christ, who is given to us and grasped by our faith."[9] The full active and passive obedience of Christ must be "credited" or "reckoned" to the sinner in order to be justified (cf. Rom. 4:3-24; 5:12-21; 2 Cor. 5:17-21).

Commenting on 2 Corinthians 5:21, Calvin notes, "We see that our righteousness is not in ourselves, but in Christ; and that all our title to it rests solely on our being partakers of Christ; for in possessing him, we possess all his riches with him."[10] This is what has been called "The Great Exchange"—the unrighteousness of sinners exchanged for the perfect righteousness of Christ. Without the divine righteousness credited to us, we are as good as dead! Robert Traill observes:

> There can be no justification without a righteousness; no righteousness can suffice but that which answers full and perfectly the holy law of God; no such righteousness can be performed but by a divine person; no benefit can accrue to a sinner by it unless it is in some way his and applied to him; no application can be made of this but by faith in Jesus Christ.[11]

Justified by Faith Alone

Very early in the formulation of Luther's thought, he maintained that "it ought to be the first concern of every Christian to lay aside all confidence in works and increasingly to strengthen faith alone and through faith to grow in the

---

[9] Martin Luther, "Lectures on Galatians (1535)" in *Luther's Works*, vol. 26 (Saint Louis: Concordia, 1963), 235.

[10] This volume, ch. 1, xxiii.

[11] Robert Traill, *Justification Vindicated* (1692; reprint, Edinburgh: Banner of Truth, 2002), 67.

knowledge, not of works, but of Christ Jesus, who suffered and rose for him."[12] This truth lies at the crux of *sola fide*—"faith alone." On the distinction of the word "alone," Calvin comments: "That a man is justified by faith, [the Papists] do not deny, because the Scripture so often declares it. But since it is nowhere expressly said to be by faith *only*, they cannot bear this addition to be made."[13] But does the Bible maintain that believers are justified by faith alone?

Calvin immediately darts to Romans 3, noting that "righteousness is manifested without the law" (v. 21), that we are "justified freely by his grace" (v. 24), and "justified without the deeds of the law" (v. 28). In other words, no act of a sinner's self-righteousness or obedience can merit God's judicial act. Elsewhere, Calvin clarifies, "When [Paul] tells us that we are justified by faith because we cannot be justified by works, he takes for granted what is true, that we cannot be justified through the righteousness of Christ unless we are poor and destitute of our own righteousness. Consequently we have to ascribe either nothing or everything to faith or to works."[14] Even if the word "alone" does not appear in the Scriptures verbatim, the *concept* is plainly there.

Eighty years after Calvin's death, his spiritual grandchildren penned the Westminster Confession of Faith—a full-bodied exposition of the Reformed Faith. In distilling the essence of the doctrine of justification, the Shorter Catechism asserts, "Justification is an act of God's free grace, wherein he

---

[12] Martin Luther, "The Freedom of a Christian" in *Three Treatises* (Philadelphia: Fortress Press, 1970), 281.

[13] This volume, ch. 1, xix.

[14] John Calvin, *The Epistles of Paul The Apostle to the Galatians, Ephesians, Philippians and Colossians*, trans. T.H.L. Parker, eds. David W. Torrance and Thomas F. Torrance (Grand Rapids: Eerdmans, 1965), 39–40.

pardoneth all our sins, and accepteth us as righteous in his sight, only for the righteousness of Christ imputed to us, and received by faith alone."

In the end, the battle over justification is not arbitrary. It is not secondary. It is ground zero. In every generation, and even today, multitudinous attacks are launched against *sola fide*. Writing in the nineteenth century, James Buchanan remarked: "When old truths are attacked with new weapons they must be vindicated by new defences, adapted to meet the most present forms of error; and this is pre-eminently the case at the present day with the cardinal doctrine of justification."[15] Well, this sentiment is as current as tomorrow's newspaper. However, as present-day warriors for justification contend earnestly, we would do well to sharpen old swords to use for the battle.

The Reason for This Volume
In preparing to preach through Paul's letter to the Galatians, I immersed myself in all-things *justification*. I wanted to read the best and brightest minds on the topic. As I began to gather secondary resources, I was directed to John Calvin's own writing on the topic of justification in his *Institutes of the Christian Religion*, and it occurred to me that a standalone volume may prove helpful to the church at large. While Martin Luther is often credited with re-discovering the doctrine of justification, it was Calvin who more fully explored the depths of this doctrine, giving it a thorough treatment.

This present volume consists of Calvin's chapters (11–19) on justification from Book 3 of his *Institutes*. The final chapter, "On Christian Liberty," may seem out of place on a book

---

[15] Buchanan, *Justification*, 9.

INTRODUCTION

strictly about justification, but I have included it, as Calvin himself calls it "an appendix to justification," which functions as the application of the doctrine. As for the translation, I have chosen to use John Allen's immensely readable edition that is readily available online, yet currently out of print.

Since many today are very familiar with Calvin's writing, I would not presume to be offering anything new or novel. Rather, my hope is to reacquaint the reader with an old friend in a new voice—gently edited and formatted to modern convention. Further, for those who may never have read Calvin's *Institutes*, this volume may be a welcome introduction to, perhaps, the key architect in the Reformed tradition.

May you be challenged and enriched, and fall even more deeply in love with the God who justifies sinners by His grace through faith in Jesus Christ.

Soli Deo Gloria!
Nate Pickowicz
Gilmanton Iron Works, NH
September 2018

1

Justification by Faith
The Name and Thing Defined

I. The Need for Discussing Justification

I think I have already explained,[1] with sufficient care, how that men, being subject to the curse of the law, have no means left of attaining salvation but through faith alone; and also what faith itself is, what Divine blessings it confers on man, and what effects it produces in him. The substance of what I have advanced is that Christ, being given to us by the goodness of God, is apprehended and possessed by us by faith, by a participation of whom we receive especially two benefits.

In the first place, being by his innocence reconciled to God, we have in heaven a propitious father instead of a judge. In the next place, being sanctified by his Spirit, we devote ourselves to innocence and purity of life. Of regeneration, which is the second benefit, I have said what I thought was sufficient. The method of justification has been but slightly touched, because it was necessary first to understand that the faith by which alone we attain gratuitous justification through the Divine mercy is

---

[1] See Calvin's *Institutes*, 2:6–7 & 3:1–10.

not unattended with good works, and what is the nature of the good works of the saints, in which part of this question consists.

The subject of justification, therefore, must now be fully discussed, and discussed with the recollection that it is the principal hinge by which religion is supported, in order that we may apply to it with the greater attention and care. For unless we first of all apprehend in what situation we stand with respect to God, and what his judgment is concerning us, we have no foundation either for a certainty of salvation, or for the exercise of piety towards God. But the necessity of knowing this subject will be more evident from the knowledge itself.

II. The Explanation of the Expressions

But that we may not stumble at the threshold (which would be the case were we to enter on a disputation concerning a subject not understood by us), let us first explain the meaning of these expressions: *To be justified in the sight of God*; and, *To be justified by faith* or *by works*.

He is said to be *justified in the sight of God* who, in the Divine judgment, is reputed righteous, and accepted on account of his righteousness. For as iniquity is abominable to God, so no sinner can find favor in his sight, as a sinner, or so long as he is considered as such. Wherever sin is, therefore, it is accompanied with the wrath and vengeance of God. He is justified who is considered not as a sinner, but as a righteous person, and on that account stands in safety before the tribunal of God, where all sinners are confounded and ruined. As if an innocent man be brought under an accusation before the tribunal of a just judge, when judgment is passed according to his innocence, he is said to be justified or acquitted before the judge; so he is justified before God who, not being numbered among sinners, has God for a witness and asserter of his righteousness.

Thus he must be said, therefore, to be *justified by works*, whose life discovers such purity and holiness, as to deserve the character of righteousness before the throne of God; or who, by the integrity of his works, can answer and satisfy the divine judgment. On the other hand, he will be *justified by faith* who, being excluded from the righteousness of works, apprehends by faith the righteousness of Christ, invested in which, he appears in the sight of God not as a sinner, but as a righteous man. Thus we simply explain justification to be: *an acceptance by which God receives us into his favor, and esteems us as righteous persons; and we say that it consists in the remission of sins and the imputation of the righteousness of Christ.*

III. *Justification*—Variously Explained

For the confirmation of this point there are many plain testimonies of Scripture. In the first place, that this is the proper and most usual signification of the word cannot be denied. But since it would be too tedious to collect all the passages and compare them together, let it suffice to have suggested it to the reader, for he will easily observe it of himself. I will only produce a few places where this justification of which we speak is expressly handled.

First, where Luke relates that "the people that heard Christ justified God," and where Christ pronounces that "wisdom is justified of all her children" (Luke 7:29, 35). *To justify God*, in the former passage, does not signify to confer righteousness, which always remains perfect in him, although the whole world endeavor to rob him of it. Nor, in the latter passage, does the *justifying of wisdom* denote making the doctrine of salvation righteous, which is so of itself. But both passages imply an ascription to God and to his doctrine of the praise which they deserve.

Again, when Christ reprehends the Pharisees for "justifying themselves" (Luke 16:15), he does not mean that they attained righteousness by doing what was right, but that they ostentatiously endeavored to gain the character of righteousness of which they were destitute. This is better understood by persons who are skilled in the Hebrew language, which gives the appellation of *sinners*, not only to those who are conscious to themselves of sin, but to persons who fall under a sentence of condemnation. For Bathsheba, when she says, "I and my son Solomon shall be counted offenders," or sinners (1 Kings 1:21), confesses no crime, but complains that she and her son will be exposed to the disgrace of being numbered among condemned criminals. And it appears from the context that this word, even in the translation, cannot be understood in any other than a relative sense, and that it does not denote the real character.

But with respect to the present subject, where Paul says, "The Scripture foresaw that God would justify the heathen through faith" (Gal. 3:8), what can we understand but that God imputes righteousness through faith? Again, when he says that God "justifies the ungodly which believes in Jesus" (Rom. 3:26; 4:5), what can be the meaning, but that he delivers him by the blessing of faith from the condemnation deserved by his ungodliness? He speaks still more plainly in the conclusion when he thus exclaims: "Who shall lay anything to the charge of God's elect? It is God that justifies. Who is he that condemns? It is Christ that died, yea rather, that is risen again, who also makes intercession for us" (Rom. 8:33–34). For it is just as if he had said, "Who shall accuse them whom God absolves? Who shall condemn those for whom Christ intercedes?" Justification, therefore, is no other than an acquittal from guilt of him who was accused, as though his innocence had been proved. Since God, therefore, justifies us through the mediation of Christ, he acquits us, not by an admission of our personal innocence, but by an imputation of righteousness; so that we, who are unrighteous in ourselves, are considered as righteous in Christ.

This is the doctrine preached by Paul in the thirteenth chapter of the Acts: "Through this man is preached unto you the forgiveness of sins; and by him all that believe are justified from all things, from which you could not be justified by the law of Moses" (Acts 13:38-39). We see that, after remission of sins, this justification is mentioned, as if by way of explanation. We see clearly that it means an acquittal; that it is separated from the works of the law; that it is a mere favor of Christ; that it is apprehended by faith. We see, finally, the interposition of a satisfaction when he says that we are justified from sins by Christ. Thus, when it is said that the publican "went down to his house justified" (Luke 18:14), we cannot say that he obtained righteousness by any merit of works. The meaning therefore is that, after he had obtained the pardon of his sins, he was considered as righteous in the sight of God. He was righteous, therefore, not through any approbation of his works, but through God's gracious absolution. Wherefore Ambrose beautifully styles confession of sins, a legitimate justification.

IV. Other Expressions of Justification

But leaving all contention about the term, if we attend to the thing itself, as it is described to us, every doubt will be removed. For Paul certainly describes justification as an acceptance when he says to the Ephesians, "God has predestinated us to the adoption of children by Jesus Christ to himself, according to the good pleasure of his will, to the praise of the glory of his grace, wherein he has made us accepted" (Eph. 1:5-6). The meaning of this passage is the same as when, in another place, we are said to be "justified freely by his grace" (Rom. 3:24).

But in the fourth chapter to the Romans, he first mentions an imputation of righteousness, and immediately represents it as consisting in remission of sins. "David," says he, "describes the blessedness of the man unto whom God imputes righteousness without works, saying, 'Blessed are they whose iniquities are forgiven,'" &c. (Rom. 4:6-8). He there, indeed, argues not concerning a branch, but the whole of justification. He also adduces the definition of it given by David, when he pronounces them to be blessed who receive the free forgiveness of their sins; whence it appears that this righteousness of which he speaks is simply opposed to guilt.

But the most decisive passage of all on this point is where he teaches us that the grand object of the ministry of the gospel is that we may "be reconciled to God," because he is pleased to receive us into his favor through Christ, "not imputing" our "trespasses unto" us (2 Cor. 5:18-19). Let the reader carefully examine the whole context. For when, by way of explanation, he just after adds, in order to describe the method of reconciliation, that Christ, "who knew no sin," was "made sin for us" (2 Cor. 5:21), he undoubtedly means by the term "reconciliation," no other than justification. Nor would there be any truth in what he affirms in another place, that we are "made righteous by the obedience of Christ" (Rom. 5:19), unless we are reputed righteous before God, in him, and out of ourselves.

V. Refuting Osiander on *Essential Righteousness*

But since Osiander[2] has introduced I know not what monstrous notion of essential righteousness, by which, though he had no intention to destroy justification by grace, yet he has involved it in such obscurity as darkens pious minds, and deprives them of a serious sense of the grace of Christ,—it will be worthwhile, before I pass to anything else, to refute this idle notion.

In the first place, this speculation is the mere fruit of insatiable curiosity. He accumulates, indeed, many testimonies of Scripture to prove that Christ is one with us, and we one with him, of which there is no proof necessary; but for want of observing the bond of this union, he bewilders himself. For us, however, who hold that we are united to Christ by the secret energy of his Spirit, it will be easy to obviate all his sophisms. He had conceived a notion similar to what was held by the Manichæans,[3] so that he wished to transfuse the Divine essence into men. Hence another discovery of his that Adam was formed in the image of God, because, even antecedently to the fall, Christ had been appointed the exemplar of the human nature. But for the sake of brevity, I shall only insist on the subject now before us. He says that we are one with Christ. This we admit;

---

[2] Andreas Osiander (1498-1552) was a German Lutheran theologian and mystic. In his brief evaluation of Osiander, Louis Berkhof writes, "Osiander revealed a tendency to revive in the Lutheran Church the essentials of the Roman Catholic conception of justification, though with a characteristic difference. He asserted that justification does not consist in the imputation of the vicarious righteousness of Christ to the sinner, but in the implanting of a new principle of life. According to him the righteousness by which we are justified is the eternal righteousness of God the Father, which is imparted to or infused into us by His Son Jesus Christ." *Systematic Theology* (Grand Rapids: Eerdmans, 1939), 525.

[3] A mystic religion founded in the second century by an Iranian Gnostic named Mani.

but we at the same time deny that Christ's essence is blended with ours.

In the next place, we assert that this principle—that Christ is our righteousness because he is the eternal God, the fountain of righteousness, and the essential righteousness of God—is grossly perverted to support his fallacies. The reader will excuse me if I now just hint at these things, which the order of the treatise requires to be deferred to another place. But though he alleges, in vindication of himself, that by the term *essential righteousness* he only intends to oppose the opinion that we are reputed righteous for the sake of Christ, yet he manifestly shows that, not content with that righteousness which has been procured for us by the obedience and sacrificial death of Christ, he imagines that we are substantially righteous in God by the infusion of his essence as well as his character. For this is the reason why he so vehemently contends that, not only Christ, but the Father and the Holy Spirit also dwell in us; which, though I allow it to be a truth, yet I maintain that he has grossly perverted. For he ought to have fully considered the nature of this inhabitation, namely, that the Father and the Spirit are in Christ, and that as "all the fullness of the Godhead dwells in him" (Col. 2:9), so in him we possess the whole Deity. Whatever, therefore, he advances concerning the Father and the Spirit separately has no other tendency but to seduce the simple from Christ.

In the next place, he introduces a mixture of substances, by which God, transfusing himself into us, makes us, as it were, a part of himself. For he considers it as of no importance that the power of the Holy Spirit unites us to Christ, so that he becomes our head and we become his members, unless his essence be blended with ours. But when speaking of the Father and the Spirit, he more openly betrays his opinion; which is, that we are not justified by the sole grace of the Mediator, and that righteousness is not simply or really offered to us in his person; but that we are made partakers of the Divine righteousness when God is essentially united with us.

VI. On the Necessity of the Refutation

If he had only said that Christ, in justifying us, becomes ours by an essential union, and that he is our head not only as man, but that the essence of his Divine nature also is infused into us, he might have entertained himself with his fancies with less mischief, nor perhaps would so great a contention have been excited about this reverie. But as this principle is like a cuttlefish, which, by the emission of black and turbid blood conceals its many tails, there is a necessity for a vigorous opposition to it, unless we mean to submit to be openly robbed of that righteousness which alone affords us any confidence concerning our salvation. For throughout this discussion the terms *righteousness* and *justify* are extended by him to two things.

First, he understands that "to be justified" denotes not only to be reconciled to God by a free pardon, but also to be made righteous; and that righteousness is not a gratuitous imputation, but a sanctity and integrity inspired by the Divine essence which resides in us. Secondly, he resolutely denies that Christ is our righteousness, as having, in the character of a priest, expiated our sins and appeased the Father on our behalf, but as being the eternal God and everlasting life. To prove the first assertion, that God justifies not only by pardoning but also by regenerating, he inquires whether God leaves those whom he justifies in their natural state without any reformation of their manners.

The answer is very easy; as Christ cannot be divided, so these two blessings, which we receive together in him, are also inseparable. Whomsoever, therefore, God receives into his favor, he likewise gives them the Spirit of adoption, by whose power he renews them in his own image. But if the brightness of the sun be inseparable from his heat, shall we therefore say that the earth is warmed by his light and illuminated by his heat? Nothing can be more apposite to the present subject than this similitude. The beams of the sun quicken and fertilize the earth, his rays brighten and illuminate it. Here is a mutual and indivisible connection. Yet reason itself prohibits us to transfer to one what is peculiar to the other.

In this confusion of two blessings, which Osiander obtrudes on us, there is a similar absurdity. For as God actually renews to the practice of righteousness those whom he gratuitously accepts as righteous, Osiander confounds that gift of regeneration with this gracious acceptance, and contends that they are one and the same. But the Scripture, though it connects them together, yet enumerates them distinctly, that the manifold grace of God may be the more evident to us. For that passage of Paul is not superfluous, that "Christ is made unto us righteousness and sanctification" (1 Cor. 1:30). And whenever he argues, from the salvation procured for us, from the paternal love of God, and from the grace of Christ, that we are called to holiness and purity, he plainly indicates that it is one thing to be justified and another thing to be made new creatures.

When Osiander appeals to the Scripture, he corrupts as many passages as he cites. The assertion of Paul that "to him that works not, but believes on him that justifies the ungodly, his faith is counted for righteousness" (Rom. 4:5), is explained by Osiander to denote making a man righteous. With the same temerity he corrupts the whole of that fourth chapter to the Romans, and hesitates not to impose the same false gloss on the passage just cited, "Who shall lay anything to the charge of God's elect? It is God that justifies"—where it is evident that the apostle is treating simply of accusation and absolution, and that his meaning wholly rests on the antithesis. His folly, therefore, betrays itself both in his arguments and in his citations of Scripture proofs.

With no more propriety does he treat of the word *righteousness* when he says, "that faith was reckoned to Abraham for righteousness," because that after having embraced Christ (who is the righteousness of God, and God himself), he was eminent for the greatest virtues. Whence it appears that, of two good parts, he erroneously makes one corrupt whole. For the righteousness there mentioned does not belong to the whole course of Abraham's life, but rather the Spirit testifies that notwithstanding the singular eminence of Abraham's virtues, and his laudable and persevering advancement in them, yet he did not please God any otherwise than in receiving by faith the grace offered in the promise. Whence it follows that, in justification, there is no regard paid to works, as Paul conclusively argues in that passage.

VII. Further Arguments Surrounding Faith

His objection that the power of justifying belongs not to faith of itself, but only as it receives Christ, I readily admit. For if faith were to justify of itself, or by an intrinsic efficacy, as it is expressed, being always weak and imperfect, it never could effect this but in part; and thus it would be a defective justification, which would only confer on us a partial salvation. Now, we entertain no such notion as the objection supposes. On the contrary, we affirm that, strictly speaking, "it is God that justifies;" and then we transfer this to Christ, because he is given to us for righteousness. Faith we compare to a vessel; for unless we come empty with the mouth of our soul open to implore the grace of Christ, we cannot receive Christ.

Whence, it may be inferred, that we do not detract from Christ the power of justifying when we teach that faith receives him before it receives his righteousness. Nevertheless, I cannot admit the intricate comparisons of this sophist when he says that faith is Christ, as though an earthen vessel were a treasure because gold is concealed in it. For faith, although intrinsically it is of no dignity or value, justifies us by an application of Christ, just as a vessel full of money constitutes a man rich. Therefore I maintain that faith, which is only the instrument by which righteousness is received, cannot without absurdity be confounded with Christ who is the material cause, and at once the author and dispenser of so great a benefit. We have now removed the difficulty as to the sense in which the word faith ought to be understood, when it is applied to justification.

VIII. Arguments on the Partaking in Christ's Righteousness

Respecting the reception of Christ, he goes still greater lengths, asserting that the internal word is received by the ministry of the external word, by which he would divert us from the priesthood of Christ and the person of the Mediator to his eternal divinity. We do not divide Christ, but we maintain that the same person who, by reconciling us to the Father in his own flesh, has given us righteousness, is the eternal Word of God; and we confess that he could not otherwise have discharged the office of Mediator, and procured righteousness for us, if he were not the eternal God.

The Name and Thing Defined

But the opinion of Osiander is that, since Christ is both God and man, he is made righteousness to us in respect of his Divine, not his human nature. Now, if this properly belong to the Divinity, it will not be peculiar to Christ, but common also to the Father and the Spirit, since the righteousness of one is the same as that of the others. Besides, what has been naturally eternal cannot with propriety be said to be "made unto us." But though we grant that God is made righteousness unto us, how will it agree with the clause which is inserted that "of God," he "is made unto us righteousness?" This is certainly peculiar to the character of the Mediator who, though he contains in himself the Divine nature, yet is designated by this appropriate title by which he is distinguished from the Father and the Spirit.

But he ridiculously triumphs in that single expression of Jeremiah, where he promises that "the Lord," *Jehovah* will be "our righteousness" (Jer. 23:6; 33:16). He can deduce nothing from this but that Christ, who is our righteousness, is God manifested in the flesh. We have elsewhere recited from Paul's sermon that "God has purchased the Church with his own blood" (Acts 20:28). If any should infer from this that the blood by which our sins were expiated was Divine, and part of the Divine nature, who could bear so monstrous an error? But Osiander thinks he has gained everything by this very puerile[4] cavil; he swells, exults, and fills many pages with his swelling words, though the passage is simply and readily explained by saying that, Jehovah, when he should become the seed of David, would be the righteousness of the pious; and in the same sense Isaiah informs us, "by his knowledge shall my righteous servant justify many" (Isa. 53:11). Let us remark that the speaker here is

---

[4] Childish.

the Father; that he attributes to his Son the office of justifying; that he adds as a reason, that he is righteous; and that he places the mode or means of effecting this in the doctrine by which Christ is made known. For it is more suitable to understand the [Hebrew] word *da'ath* in a passive sense.

Hence I conclude, first, that Christ was made righteousness when he assumed the form of a servant. Secondly, that he justifies us by his own obedience to the Father; and, therefore, that he does this for us, not according to his Divine nature, but by reason of the dispensation committed to him. For though God alone is the fountain of righteousness, and we are righteous only by a participation of him, yet because we have been alienated from his righteousness through the unhappy breach occasioned by the Fall, we are under the necessity of descending to this inferior remedy, to be justified by Christ, by the efficacy of his death and resurrection.

IX. Arguments Pertaining to the Divine Nature

If Osiander object that the excellence of this work surpasses the nature of man, and therefore can be ascribed only to the Divine nature,—the former part of the objection I admit, but in the latter I maintain that he is grossly mistaken. For although Christ could neither purify our souls with his blood, nor appease the Father by his sacrifice, nor absolve us from guilt, nor, in short, perform the functions of a priest, if he were not truly God, because human power would have been unequal to so great a burden, yet it is certain that he performed all these things in his human nature.

For if it be inquired, how are we justified? Paul replies, "By the obedience" of Christ (Rom. 5:19). But has he obeyed in any other way than by assuming the form of a servant? Hence we infer that righteousness is presented to us in his flesh. In the other passage also, which I much wonder that Osiander is not ashamed to quote so frequently, Paul places the source of righteousness wholly in the humanity of Christ. "He has made him to be sin for us, who knew no sin, that we might be made the righteousness of God in him" (2 Cor. 5:21). Osiander lays great stress on "the righteousness of God," and triumphs as though he had evinced it to be his notion of essential righteousness; whereas the words convey a very different idea,—that we are righteous through the expiation effected by Christ.

That "the righteousness of God" means that which God approves ought to have been known to the youngest novices, just as in John "the praise of God" is opposed to "the praise of men" (John 12:43). I know that "the righteousness of God" sometimes denotes that of which he is the author, and which he bestows upon us; but without any observation of mine, the judicious reader will perceive that the meaning of this passage is only that we stand before the tribunal of God supported by the atoning death of Christ. Nor is the term of such great importance, provided that Osiander coincides with us in this, that we are justified in Christ, inasmuch as he was made an expiatory sacrifice for us, which is altogether incompatible with his Divine nature. For this reason, when Christ designs to seal the righteousness and salvation which he has presented to us, he exhibits a certain pledge of it in his flesh. He calls himself, indeed, "living bread;" but adds, by way of explanation, "my flesh is meat indeed, and my blood is drink indeed." This method of instruction is discovered in the sacraments; which, although they direct our faith to the whole of the person of Christ, not to a part of him only, yet at the same time teach that the matter of justification and salvation resides in his human nature; not that he either justifies or vivifies, of himself as a mere man, but because it has pleased God to manifest in the Mediator that which was incomprehensible and hidden in himself.

Wherefore I am accustomed to say that Christ is, as it were, a fountain opened to us, whence we may draw what were otherwise concealed and useless in that secret and deep fountain which flows to us in the person of the Mediator. In this manner, and in this sense, provided he will submit to the clear and forcible arguments which I have adduced, I do not deny that Christ justifies us, as he is God and man, and that this work is common also to the Father and the Spirit; and, finally, that the righteousness of which Christ makes us partakers is the eternal righteousness of the eternal God.

X. Christ as Our Righteousness

Moreover, that his cavils may not deceive the inexperienced, I confess that we are destitute of this incomparable blessing, till Christ becomes ours. I attribute, therefore, the highest importance to the connection between the head and members; to the inhabitation of Christ in our hearts; in a word, to the mystical union by which we enjoy him, so that being made ours, he makes us partakers of the blessings with which he is furnished. We do not, then, contemplate him at a distance out of ourselves, that his righteousness may be imputed to us; but because we have put him on, and are grafted into his body, and because he has deigned to unite us to himself, therefore we glory in a participation of his righteousness.

Thus we refute the cavil of Osiander that faith is considered by us as righteousness; as though we despoiled Christ of his

The Name and Thing Defined

right when we affirm that, by faith we come to him empty; that he alone may fill us with his grace. But Osiander, despising this spiritual connection, insists on a gross mixture of Christ with believers, and therefore invidiously gives the appellation of Zwinglians to all who do not subscribe to his fanatical error concerning essential righteousness; because they are not of opinion that Christ is substantially eaten in the sacred supper. As for myself, indeed, I consider it the highest honor to be thus reproached by a man so proud and so absorbed in his own delusions; although he attacks not me alone, but other writers well known in the world whom he ought to have treated with modest respect. But this does not at all affect me, who am supporting no private interest; wherefore I the more unreservedly advocate this cause, conscious that I am free from every sinister motive.

His great importunity in insisting on essential righteousness, and an essential inhabitation of Christ in us, goes to this length—first, that God transfuses himself into us by a gross mixture of himself with us, as he pretends that there is a carnal eating in the sacred supper; secondly, that God inspires his righteousness into us, by which we are really righteous with him, since, according to this man, such righteousness is as really God himself, as the goodness, or holiness, or perfection of God. I shall not take much trouble to refute the testimonies adduced by him, which he violently perverts from the celestial to the present state. By Christ, says Peter, "are given unto us exceeding great and precious promises; that by these you might be partakers of the Divine nature" (2 Pet. 1:4). As though we were now such as the gospel promises we shall be at the second advent of Christ; nay, John apprizes us that then "we shall be like God; for we shall see him as he is" (1 John 3:2). I have thought proper to give the reader only a small specimen, and endeavored to pass over these impertinences, not that it is difficult to refute them, but because I am unwilling to be tedious in laboring to no purpose.

XI. Osiander's Confusion Regarding Imputation

There is yet more latent poison in the second particular, in which he maintains that we are righteous together with God. I think I have already sufficiently demonstrated that, although this dogma were not so pestiferous, yet because it is weak and unsatisfactory and evaporates through its own inanity, it ought justly to be rejected by all judicious and pious readers. But this is an impiety not to be tolerated—under the pretext of a twofold righteousness to weaken the assurance of salvation, and to elevate us above the clouds, that we may not embrace by faith the grace of expiation, and call upon God with tranquility of mind. Osiander ridicules those who say that justification is a forensic term, because it is necessary for us to be actually righteous; nor is there anything that he more dislikes than the doctrine that we are justified by gratuitous imputation. Now, if God does not justify by absolving and pardoning us, what is the meaning of this declaration of Paul? "God was in Christ, reconciling the world unto himself, not imputing their trespasses unto them. For he has made him to be sin for us, who knew no sin; that we might be made the righteousness of God in him" (2 Cor. 5:19, 21).

First, I find that they are accounted righteous who are reconciled to God. The manner is specified, that God justifies by pardoning; just as, in another passage, justification is opposed to accusation; which antithesis clearly demonstrates that the form of expression is borrowed from the practice of courts. Nor is there any one, but tolerably versed in the Hebrew language, provided at the same time that he be in his sound senses, who can be ignorant that this is the original of the phrase, and that this is its import and meaning. Now, let Osiander answer me whether, where Paul says that "David describes righteousness without works, saying. 'Blessed are they whose iniquities are forgiven,'" (Rom. 4:6–8), whether, I say, this be a complete definition or a partial one. Certainly Paul does not adduce the testimony of the Psalmist, as teaching that pardon of sins is a part of righteousness, or concurs to the justification of a man. But he includes the whole of righteousness in a free remission, pronouncing, "Blessed are they whose iniquities are forgiven, and whose sins are covered. Blessed is the man to whom the Lord will not impute sin." He thence estimates and judges of the felicity of such a man, because in this way, he becomes righteous, not actually, but by imputation. Osiander objects, that it would be dishonorable to God, and contrary to his nature, if he justified those who still remain actually impious.

But it should be remembered that, as I have already observed, the grace of justification is inseparable from regeneration, although they are distinct things. But since it is sufficiently known from experience, that some relics of sin always remain in the righteous, the manner of their justification must of necessity be very different from that of their renovation to newness of life. For the latter God commences in his elect, and as long as they live carries it on gradually, and sometimes slowly, so that they are always obnoxious at his tribunal to the sentence of death. He justifies them, however, not in a partial manner, but so completely that they may boldly appear in heaven, as being invested with the purity of Christ. For no portion of righteousness could satisfy our consciences, till we have ascertained that God is pleased with us, as being unexceptionably righteous before him. Whence it follows that the doctrine of justification is perverted and totally overturned, when doubts are injected into the mind, when the confidence of salvation is shaken, when bold and fearless worship is interrupted, and when quiet and tranquility with spiritual joy are not established.

Whence Paul argues from the incompatibility of things contrary to each other, that the inheritance is not of the law, because then faith would be rendered vain (Gal. 3:18); which, if it be fixed upon works, must inevitably fall; since not even the most holy of all saints will find them afford any ground of confidence. This difference between justification and regeneration (which Osiander confounds together, and denominates a twofold righteousness) is beautifully expressed by Paul; for, speaking of his real righteousness, or of the integrity which he possessed, to which Osiander gives the appellation of essential righteousness, he sorrowfully exclaims, "O wretched man that I am! who shall deliver me from the body of this death" (Rom. 7:24)? But resorting to the righteousness which is founded in the Divine mercy alone, he nobly triumphs over life, and death, and reproaches, and famine, and the sword, and all adverse things and persons. "Who shall lay anything to the charge of God's elect? It is God that justifies. For I am persuaded that nothing shall be able to separate us from the love of God, which is in Christ Jesus our Lord" (Rom. 8:33, 38-39). He plainly declares himself to be possessed of that righteousness, which alone is fully sufficient for salvation in the sight of God; so that the miserable servitude, in a consciousness of which he was just before bewailing his condition, neither diminishes nor in the smallest degree interrupts, the confidence with which he triumphs. This diversity is sufficiently known, and is even familiar to all the saints, who groan under the burden of their iniquities, and yet with victorious confidence rise superior to every fear.

But the objection of Osiander, that it is incongruous to the nature of God, recoils upon himself; for, although he invests the saints with a twofold righteousness, as with a garment covered with skins, he is, notwithstanding, constrained to acknowledge that no man can please God without the remission of his sins. If this be true, he should at least grant that they who are not actually righteous are accounted righteous in proportion, as it is expressed, to the degree of imputation. But how far shall a sinner extend this gracious acceptance, which is substituted in the place of righteousness? Shall he estimate it by the weight? Truly he will be in great uncertainty to which side to incline the balance, because he will not be able to assume to himself as much righteousness as may be necessary to his confidence. It is well that he, who would wish to prescribe laws to God, is not the arbiter of this cause. But this address of David to God will remain: "That you might be justified when you speak, and be clear when you judge" (Psa. 51:5). And what extreme arrogance it is to condemn the supreme Judge when he freely absolves, and not to be satisfied with this answer, "I will show mercy on whom I will show mercy" (Exod. 33:19)! And yet the intercession of Moses, which God checked with this reply, was not that he would spare none, but that, though they were guilty, he would remove their guilt and absolve them all at once. We affirm, therefore, that those who were undone are justified before God by the obliteration of their sins; because, sin being the object of his hatred, he can love none but those whom he justifies. But this is a wonderful method of justification, that sinners, being invested with the righteousness of Christ, dread not the judgment which they have deserved; and that, while they justly condemn themselves, they are accounted righteous out of themselves.

XII. Continued Errors of Osiander

But the readers must be cautioned to pay a strict attention to the mystery which Osiander boasts, that he will not conceal from them. For, after having contended with great prolixity, that we do not obtain favor with God solely through the imputation of the righteousness of Christ, because it would be impossible for him to esteem those as righteous who are not so (I use his own words), he at length concludes that Christ is given to us for righteousness, not in respect of his human, but of his Divine nature; and that, though this righteousness can only be found in the person of the Mediator, yet it is the righteousness, not of man, but of God. He does not combine two righteousnesses, but evidently deprives the humanity of Christ of all concern in the matter of justification.

It is worthwhile, however, to hear what arguments he adduces. It is said in the passage referred to, that "Christ is made unto us wisdom" (1 Cor. 1:30), which is applicable only to the eternal Word. Neither, therefore, is Christ, considered as man our righteousness. I reply, that the only begotten Son of God was indeed his eternal wisdom; but this title is here ascribed to him by Paul in a different sense, because "in him are hid all the treasures of wisdom and knowledge" (Col. 2:3). What, therefore, he had with the Father, he has manifested to us; and so what Paul says refers not to the essence of the Son of God, but to our benefit, and is rightly applied to the humanity of Christ; because, although he was a light shining in darkness before his assumption of the flesh, yet he was a hidden light till he appeared in the nature of man "as the Sun of righteousness" (Mal. 4:2); wherefore he calls himself "the light of the world" (John 8:12).

Osiander betrays his folly likewise in objecting that justification exceeds the power of angels and men, since it depends not upon the dignity of any creature, but upon the appointment of God. If angels were desirous to offer a satisfaction to God, it would be unavailing, because they have not been appointed to it. This was peculiar to the man Christ, who was "made under the law, to redeem us from the curse of the law" (Gal. 3:13; 4:4). He likewise very unjustly accuses those who deny that Christ is our righteousness according to his Divine nature, of retaining only one part of Christ, and (what is worse) making two Gods; because, though they acknowledge that God dwells in us, yet they flatly deny that we are righteous through the righteousness of God. For if we call Christ the author of life in consequence of his having suffered death, "that he might destroy him that had the power of death" (Heb. 2:14), it is not to be inferred that we deny this honor to his complete person, as God manifested in the flesh: we only state with precision the means by which the righteousness of God is conveyed to us, so that we may enjoy it. In this Osiander has fallen into a very pernicious error. We do not deny that what is openly exhibited to us in Christ flows from the secret grace and power of God, nor do we refuse to admit that the righteousness conferred on us by Christ is the righteousness of God as proceeding from him. But we constantly maintain that we have righteousness and life in the death and resurrection of Christ.

I pass over that shameful accumulation of passages, with which, without any discrimination, and even without common sense, he has burdened the reader, in order to evince that wherever mention is made of righteousness, it ought to be understood of this essential righteousness; as where David implores the righteousness of God to assist him; which as he does above a hundred times, Osiander hesitates not to pervert such a great number of passages. Nor is there anything more solid in his other objection that the term "righteousness" is properly and rightly applied to that by which we are excited to rectitude of conduct and that God alone "works in us both to will and to do" (Phil. 2:13).

Now, we do not deny that God renews us by his Spirit to holiness and righteousness of life, but it should first be inquired whether he does this immediately by himself, or through the medium of his Son with whom he has deposited all the plenitude of his Spirit, that with his abundance he might relieve the necessities of his members. Besides, though righteousness flows to us from the secret fountain of the Divinity, yet it does not follow that Christ, who in the flesh sanctified himself for our sakes (John 17:19), is our righteousness with respect to his Divine nature. Equally frivolous in his assertion, that Christ himself was righteous with the righteousness of God; because, if he had not been influenced by the will of the Father, not even he could have performed the part assigned him. For though it has been elsewhere observed that all the merit of Christ himself flows from the mere favor of God, yet this affords no countenance to the fanciful notion with which Osiander fascinates his own eyes and those of the injudicious. For who would admit the inference that, because God is the original source of our righteousness, we are therefore essentially righteous, and have the essence of the Divine righteousness residing in us?

In redeeming the Church (Isaiah says), God "put on righteousness as a breastplate" (Isa. 59:17), but was it to spoil Christ of the armor which he had given him, and to prevent his being a perfect Redeemer? The prophet only meant that God borrowed nothing extrinsic to himself, and had no assistance in the work of our redemption. Paul has briefly intimated the same in other words, saying that he has given us salvation in order "to declare his righteousness" (Rom. 3:24-25). Nor does this at all contradict what he states in another place, "that by the obedience of one we are made righteous" (Rom. 5:19). To conclude, whoever fabricates a twofold righteousness, that wretched souls may not rely wholly and exclusively on the Divine mercy, makes Christ an object of contempt, and crowns him with plaited thorns.

XIII. The Refutation of the Sophists[5]

But as many persons imagine righteousness to be composed of faith and works, let us also prove, before we proceed, that the righteousness of faith is so exceedingly different from that of works, that if one be established, the other must necessarily be subverted. The apostle says, "I count all things but dung, that I may win Christ, and be found in him, not having mine own righteousness, which is of the law, but that which is through the faith of Christ, the righteousness which is of God by faith" (Phil. 3:8-9). Here we see a comparison of two opposites, and an implication that his own righteousness must be forsaken by him

---

[5] *Sophist*: an ancient Greek teacher, trained in rhetoric and philosophy, associated in popular thought with moral skepticism; one who reasons with clever but fallacious arguments. Calvin is making reference to the Roman Catholic apologists, those whom Luther mockingly called "the theologians of glory."

who wishes to obtain the righteousness of Christ. Wherefore, in another place, he states this to have been the cause of the ruin of the Jews, that "going about to establish their own righteousness, they have not submitted themselves unto the righteousness of God" (Rom. 10:3). If, by establishing our own righteousness, we reject the righteousness of God, then, in order to obtain the latter, the former must doubtless be entirely renounced. He conveys the same sentiment when he asserts that "boasting is excluded. By what law? of works? Nay; but by the law of faith" (Rom. 3:27). Whence it follows that, as long as there remains the least particle of righteousness in our works, we retain some cause for boasting. But if faith excludes all boasting, the righteousness of works can by no means be associated with the righteousness of faith. To this purpose he speaks so clearly in the fourth chapter to the Romans, as to leave no room for cavil or evasion. "If Abraham (says he) were justified by works, he has whereof to glory." He adds, "but" he has "not" whereof to glory "before God" (Rom. 4:2). It follows, therefore, that he was not justified by works. Then he advances another argument from two opposites. "To him that works is the reward not reckoned of grace, but of debt" (Rom. 4:4). But righteousness is attributed to faith through grace. Therefore it is not from the merit of works. Adieu, therefore, to the fanciful notion of those who imagine a righteousness compounded of faith and works.

XIV. The Confusion of the Sophists: Faith and Works

The sophists, who amuse and delight themselves with perversion of the Scripture and vain cavils, think they have found a most excellent subterfuge, when they explain *works* in these passages to mean those which men yet unregenerate perform without the grace of Christ, merely through the unassisted efforts of their own free-will; and deny that they relate to spiritual works. Thus, according to them, a man is justified both by faith and by works, only the works are not properly his own, but the gifts of Christ and the fruits of regeneration. For they say that Paul spoke in this manner, only that the Jews who relied on their own strength might be convinced of their folly in arrogating righteousness to themselves, whereas it is conferred on us solely by the Spirit of Christ, not by any exertion properly our own.

But they do not observe that in the contrast of legal and evangelical righteousness, which Paul introduces in another place, all works are excluded, by what title so ever they may be distinguished. For he teaches that this is the righteousness of the law that he who has fulfilled the command of the law shall obtain salvation (Rom. 10:5ff.); but that the righteousness of faith consists in believing that Christ has died and is risen again (Gal. 3:11). Besides, we shall see, as we proceed, in its proper place, that sanctification and righteousness are separate blessings of Christ.

Whence it follows that even spiritual works are not taken into the account when the power of justifying is attributed to faith. And the assertion of Paul, in the place just cited, that Abraham has not whereof to glory before God, since he was not justified by works, ought not to be restricted to any literal appearance or external display of virtue, or to any efforts of free-will; but though the life of the patriarch was spiritual, and almost angelic, yet his works did not possess sufficient merit to justify him before God.

XV. The Consequences of Confusing the Terms

The errors of the schoolmen, who mingle their preparations, are rather more gross. But they instill into the simple and incautious a doctrine equally corrupt, while under the pretext of the Spirit and of grace, they conceal the mercy of God, which alone can calm the terrors of the conscience. We confess, indeed, with Paul that "the doers of the law are justified before God" (Rom. 2:13). But since we are all far from being observers of the law, we conclude that those works which should be principally available to justification, afford us no assistance, because we are destitute of them.

With respect to the common Papists, or schoolmen, they are in this matter doubly deceived, both in denominating faith a certainty of conscience in expecting from God a reward of merit, and in explaining the grace of God to be, not an imputation of gratuitous righteousness, but the Spirit assisting to the pursuit of holiness. They read in the apostle, "He that comes to God must believe that he is, and that he is a rewarder of them that diligently seek him" (Heb. 11:6). But they do not consider the manner of seeking him. And that they mistake the sense of the word "grace" is evident from their writings. For Lombard represents justification by Christ as given us in two ways. He says, "The death of Christ justifies us, first, because it excites charity in our hearts, by which we are made actually righteous; secondly, because it destroys sin, by which the devil held us in captivity, so that now it cannot condemn us."[6] We see how he considers the grace of God in justification to consist in our being directed to good works by the grace of the Holy Spirit. He wished, indeed, to follow the opinion of Augustine; but he

---

[6] Peter Lombard, *The Four Books of Sentences.* vol. 3, dist. 16, c. 11.

follows him at a great distance, and even deviates considerably from a close imitation of him; for whatever he finds clearly stated by him, he obscures, and whatever he finds pure in him, he corrupts.

The schools have always been running into worse and worse errors, till at length they have precipitated themselves into a kind of Pelagianism. Nor, indeed, is the opinion of Augustine, or at least his manner of expression, to be altogether admitted. For though he excellently despoils man of all the praise of righteousness, and ascribes the whole to the grace of God, yet he refers grace to sanctification, in which we are regenerated by the Spirit to newness of life.

XVI. Justification According to Scripture

The Scripture, when speaking of the righteousness of faith, leads us to something very different. It teaches us that, being diverted from the contemplation of our own works, we should regard nothing but the mercy of God and the perfection of Christ. For it states this to be the order of justification; that from the beginning God deigns to embrace sinful man with his pure and gratuitous goodness, contemplating nothing in him to excite mercy, but his misery (for God beholds him utterly destitute of all good works), deriving from himself the motive for blessing him, that he may affect the sinner himself with a sense of his supreme goodness who, losing all confidence in his own works, rests the whole of his salvation on the Divine mercy.

This is the sentiment of faith, by which the sinner comes to the enjoyment of his salvation, when he knows from the doctrine of the gospel that he is reconciled to God; that having obtained remission of sins, he is justified by the intervention of the righteousness of Christ; and though regenerated by the

Spirit of God, he thinks on everlasting righteousness reserved for him, not in the good works to which he devotes himself, but solely in the righteousness of Christ. When all these things shall have been particularly examined, they will afford a perspicuous explication of our opinion. They will, however, be better digested in a different order from that in which they have been proposed. But it is of little importance, provided they are so connected with each other, that we may have the whole subject rightly stated and well confirmed.

XVII. Justification in Romans 10 and Galatians 3:18

Here it is proper to recall to remembrance the relation we have before stated between faith and the gospel, since the reason why faith is said *to justify* is that it receives and embraces the righteousness offered in the gospel. But its being offered by the gospel absolutely excludes all consideration of works. This Paul very clearly demonstrates on various occasions, and particularly in two passages.

In his Epistle to the Romans, contrasting the law and the gospel, he says, "Moses describes the righteousness which is of the law, that the man which does those things shall live by them. But the righteousness which is of faith speaks on this wise: That if you shall confess with your mouth the Lord Jesus, and shall believe in your heart that God has raised him from the dead, you shall be saved" (Rom. 10:5, 6, 9). Do you perceive how he thus discriminates between the law and the gospel that the former attributes righteousness to works, but the latter bestows it freely without the assistance of works? It is a remarkable passage, and may serve to extricate us from a multitude of difficulties, if we understand that the righteousness which is given us by the gospel is free from all legal conditions. This is the reason why he more than once strongly opposes the promise to the law, "If the inheritance be of the law, it is no more of promise" (Gal. 3:18); and more in the same chapter to the same purpose. It is certain that the law also has its promises. Wherefore, unless we will confess the comparison to be improper, there must be something distinct and different in the promises of the gospel.

Now, what can that be, but that they are gratuitous and solely dependent on the Divine mercy, while the promises of the law depend on the condition of works? Nor let anyone object that it is only the righteousness which men would obtrude on God from their own natural powers and free-will that is rejected; since Paul teaches it as a universal truth that the precepts of the law are unprofitable, because, not only among the vulgar, but even among the very best of men, there is not one who can fulfil them (Rom. 3:10). Love is certainly the principal branch of the law. When the Spirit of God forms us to it, why does it not constitute any part of our righteousness, but because even in the saints it is imperfect, and therefore of itself deserves no reward?

XVIII. Justification in Galatians 3:11-12

The other passage is as follows: "That no man is justified by the law in the sight of God, it is evident; for the just shall live by faith. And the law is not of faith; but the man that does them shall live in them" (Gal. 3:11-12). How could this argument be supported unless it were certain that works do not come into the account of faith, but are to be entirely separated from it? The law, he says, differs from faith. Why? Because works are required to the righteousness of the law. It follows, therefore, that works are not required to the righteousness of faith. From this statement it appears that they who are justified by faith are justified without the merit of works, and beyond the merit of works; for faith receives that righteousness which the gospel bestows; and the gospel differs from the law in this respect, that it does not confine righteousness to works, but rests it entirely on the mercy of God.

He argues in a similar manner to the Romans that "Abraham had not whereof to glory; for he believed God, and it was counted unto him for righteousness" (Rom. 4:2-3). And by way of confirmation he subjoins that then there is room for the righteousness of faith when there are no works which merit any reward. He tells us that where there are works, they receive a reward "of debt," but that what is given to faith is "of grace;" for this is the clear import of the language which he there uses. When he adds, a little after, "Therefore it is of faith" that we obtain the inheritance, in order "that it might be by grace" (Rom. 4:16), he infers that the inheritance is gratuitous, because it is received by faith. And why is this, but because faith, without any assistance of works, depends wholly on the Divine mercy? And in the same sense undoubtedly he elsewhere teaches us that "the righteousness of God without the law is manifested, being witnessed by the law and the prophets" (Rom. 3:21), because, by excluding the law, he denies that righteousness is assisted by works, or that we obtain it by working, but asserts that we come empty in order to receive it.

XIX. Rome's Objection to Justification by Faith Alone

The reader will now discover with what justice the sophists of the present day cavil at our doctrine, when we say that *a man is justified by faith only*. That a man is justified by faith, they do not deny, because the Scripture so often declares it. But since it is nowhere expressly said to be by faith *only*, they cannot bear this addition to be made.

THE NAME AND THING DEFINED

But what reply will they give to these words of Paul where he contends that "righteousness is not of faith unless it be gratuitous" (Rom. 4:2)? How can anything gratuitous consist with works? And by what cavils will they elude what he asserts in another place that in the gospel "is the righteousness of God revealed" (Rom. 1:17)? If righteousness is revealed in the gospel, it is certainly not a mutilated and partial, but a complete and perfect one. The law, therefore, has no concern in it. And respecting this exclusive particle, only, they rest on an evasion which is not only false, but glaringly ridiculous. For does not he most completely attribute everything to faith alone who denies everything to works? What is the meaning of these expressions of Paul? "Righteousness is manifested without the law," "justified freely by his grace," "justified without the deeds of the law" (Rom. 3:21, 24, 28).

Here they have an ingenious subterfuge which, though it is not of their own invention but borrowed from Origen and some of the ancients, is nevertheless very absurd. They pretend that the works excluded are the ceremonial works of the law, not the moral works. They have made such a proficiency by their perpetual disputations that they have forgotten the first elements of logic. Do they suppose the apostle to have been insane when he adduced these passages in proof of his doctrine? "The man that does them shall live in them," and "Cursed is every one that continues not in all things which are written in the book of the law to do them" (Gal. 3:10, 12). If they be in their sober senses, they will not assert that life was promised to the observers of ceremonies, and the curse denounced merely on the transgressors of them. If these places are to be understood of the moral law, it is beyond a doubt that moral works likewise are excluded from the power to justify.

To the same purpose are these arguments which he uses: "For by the law is the knowledge of sin;" consequently not righteousness. "Because the law works wrath" (Rom. 3:20; 4:15), therefore not righteousness. Since the law cannot assure our consciences, neither can it confer righteousness. Since faith is counted for righteousness, consequently righteousness is not a reward of works, but is gratuitously bestowed. Since we are justified by faith, boasting is precluded. "If there had been a law given which could have given life, verily righteousness should have been by the law. But the Scripture hath concluded all under sin, that the promise by faith of Jesus Christ might be given to them that believe" (Gal. 3:21, 22). Let them idly pretend, if they dare, that these are applicable to ceremonies, not to morals; but even children would explode such consummate impudence. We may therefore be assured that when the power of justifying is denied to the law, the whole law is included.

XX. The Foundation of Righteousness: Paul's Argument

If anyone should wonder why the apostle does not content himself with simply mentioning *works*, but says *works of the law*, the reason is obvious. For though works are so greatly esteemed, they derive their value from the Divine approbation rather than from any intrinsic excellence. For who can dare to boast to God of any righteousness of works, but what he has approved? Who can dare to claim any reward as due to them, but what he has promised? It is owing, therefore, to the Divine favor that they are accounted worthy both of the title and of the reward of righteousness; and so they are valuable, only when they are intended as acts of obedience to God.

The Name and Thing Defined

Wherefore the apostle, in another place, in order to prove that Abraham could not be justified by works, alleges that "the law was four hundred and thirty years after the covenant was confirmed" (Gal. 3:17). Ignorant persons would ridicule such an argument because there might have been righteous works before the promulgation of the law; but knowing that works have no such intrinsic worth, independently of the testimony and esteem of God, he has taken it for granted that, antecedently to the law, they had no power to justify. We know why he expressly mentions "the works of the law" when he means to deny justification by works; it is because they alone can furnish any occasion of controversy. However, he likewise excludes all works, without any limitation, as when he says, "David describes the blessedness of the man, unto whom God imputes righteousness without works" (Rom. 4:6). They cannot, therefore, by any subtleties prevent us from retaining this general exclusive particle. It is in vain, also, that they catch at another frivolous subtlety, alleging that we are justified only by that "faith which works by love" (Gal. 5:6), with a view to represent righteousness as depending on love.

We acknowledge, indeed, with Paul that no other faith justifies except that "which works by love," but it does not derive its power to justify from the efficacy of that love. It justifies in no other way than as it introduces us into a participation of the righteousness of Christ. Otherwise there would be no force in the argument so strenuously urged by the apostle. "To him that works," he says, "is the reward not reckoned of grace, but of debt. But to him that works not, but believeth on him that justifies the ungodly, his faith is counted for righteousness" (Rom. 4:4, 5). Was it possible for him to speak more plainly than by thus asserting that there is no righteousness of faith, except where there are no works entitled to any reward; and that faith is imputed for righteousness, only when righteousness is conferred through unmerited grace?

XXI. Justification Established

Now, let us examine the truth of what has been asserted in the definition, that the righteousness of faith is a reconciliation with God, which consists solely in remission of sins.[7] We must always return to this axiom—That the Divine wrath remains on all men, as long as they continue to be sinners. This Isaiah has beautifully expressed in the following words: "The Lord's hand is not shortened, that it cannot save; neither is his ear heavy, that it cannot hear; but your iniquities have separated between you and your God, and your sins have hid his face from you, that he will not hear" (Isa. 59:1, 2). We are informed that sin makes a division between man and God, and turns the Divine countenance away from the sinner. Nor can it be otherwise, because it is incompatible with his righteousness to have any communion with sin.

Hence the apostle teaches that man is an enemy to God till he be reconciled to him through Christ (Rom. 5:8-10). Whom, therefore, the Lord receives into fellowship, him he is said to justify; because he cannot receive any one into favor or into fellowship with himself without making him from a sinner to be a righteous person. This, we add, is accomplished by the remission of sins. For if they, whom the Lord has reconciled to himself, be judged according to their works, they will still be found actually sinners, who, not withstanding, must be absolved and free from sin. It appears, then, that those whom God

---

[7] Section II.

receives are made righteous no otherwise than as they are purified by being cleansed from all their defilements by the remission of their sins; so that such a righteousness may, in one word, be denominated a remission of sins.

XXII. Confirmed by Scripture and the Fathers

Both these points are fully established by the language of Paul, which I have already recited. "God was in Christ, reconciling the world unto himself, not imputing their trespasses unto them; and has committed unto us the word of reconciliation" (2 Cor. 5:19). Then he adds the substance of his ministry: "He has made him to be sin for us, who knew no sin; that we might be made the righteousness of God in him" (v. 21). The terms "righteousness" and "reconciliation" are here used by him indiscriminately to teach us that they are mutually comprehended in each other. And he states the manner of obtaining this righteousness to consist in our transgressions not being imputed to us. Wherefore we can no longer doubt how God justifies when we hear that he reconciles us to himself by not imputing our sins to us.

Thus, in the Epistle to the Romans, the apostle proves that "God imputes righteousness without works," from the testimony of David who declares, "Blessed are they whose iniquities are forgiven, and whose sins are covered. Blessed is the man to whom the Lord will not impute sin" (Rom. 4:6-8). By "blessedness," in this passage, he undoubtedly means righteousness; for since he asserts it to consist in remission of sins, there is no reason for our adopting any other definition of it. Wherefore Zachariah, the father of John the Baptist, places "the knowledge of salvation" in "the remission of sins" (Luke 1:77). And Paul, observing the same rule in the sermon which he preached to the people of Antioch on the subject of salvation, is stated by Luke to have concluded in the following manner: "Through this man is preached unto you the forgiveness of sins; and by him all that believe are justified from all things, from which you could not be justified by the law of Moses" (Acts 13:38, 39). The apostle thus connects "forgiveness of sins" with "justification" to show that they are identically the same; whence he justly argues that this righteousness which we obtain through the favor of God is gratuitously bestowed upon us.

Nor should it be thought a strange expression that believers are justified before God, not by their works, but by his gracious acceptance of them; since it occurs so frequently in the Scripture, and sometimes also in the fathers. Augustine says, "The righteousness of the saints, in this world, consists rather in the remission of their sins than in the perfection of their virtues."[8] With which corresponds the remarkable observation of Bernard: "Not to sin at all, is the righteousness of God; but the righteousness of man is the Divine grace and mercy." He had before asserted "that Christ is righteousness to us in absolution, and therefore that they alone are righteous who have obtained pardon through his mercy."[9]

XXIII. Obtaining Christ's Righteousness by Imputation

Hence, also, it is evident that we obtain justification before God solely by the intervention of the righteousness of Christ; which is equivalent to saying that a man is righteous, not in himself, but because the righteousness of Christ is communicated to him by imputation; and this is a point which deserves an attentive consideration. For it supersedes that idle notion that a man is

---

[8] Augustine, *The City of God,* vol. 19, c. 27.
[9] Bernard of Clairvaux, *Sermons on the Song of Songs,* serm. 22, 23.

justified by faith because faith receives the Spirit of God by whom he is made righteous; which is too repugnant to the foregoing doctrine, ever to be reconcilable to it. For he must certainly be destitute of all righteousness of his own, who is taught to seek a righteousness out of himself. This is most clearly asserted by the apostle when he says, "He has made him to be sin for us, who knew no sin; that we might be made the righteousness of God in him" (2 Cor. 5:21). We see that our righteousness is not in ourselves, but in Christ; and that all our title to it rests solely on our being partakers of Christ; for in possessing him, we possess all his riches with him.

Nor does any objection arise from what he states in another place that "God, sending his own Son in the likeness of sinful flesh, and for sin, condemned sin in the flesh; that the righteousness of the law might be fulfilled in us" (Rom. 8:3, 4); where he intends no other fulfilment than what we obtain by imputation. For the Lord Christ so communicates his righteousness to us that, with reference to the Divine judgment, he transfuses its virtue into us in a most wonderful manner. That the apostle intended no other, abundantly appears from another declaration, which he had made just before: "As by one man's disobedience many were made sinners, so by the obedience of one shall many be made righteous" (Rom. 5:19). What is placing our righteousness in the obedience of Christ, but asserting that we are accounted righteous only because his obedience is accepted for us as if it were our own?

Wherefore Ambrose appears to me to have very beautifully exemplified this righteousness in the benediction of Jacob; that as he, who had on his own account no claim to the privileges of primogeniture, being concealed in his brother's habit, and invested with his garment, which diffused a most excellent odor, insinuated himself into the favor of his father, that he might receive the benediction to his own advantage, under the character of another; so we shelter ourselves under the precious purity of Christ our elder brother that we may obtain the testimony of righteousness in the sight of God. The words of Ambrose are,

> That Isaac smelled the odor of the garments, perhaps indicates, that we are justified not by works, but by faith; since the infirmity of the flesh is an impediment to works, but the brightness of faith, which merits the pardon of sin, conceals the error of our actions.[10]

And such is indeed the real fact; for that we may appear before the face of God to salvation, it is necessary for us to be perfumed with his fragrance, and to have all our deformities concealed and absorbed in his perfection.

---

[10] Ambrose, *Jacob and the Happy Life,* vol. 2, c. 2.

2

A Consideration of the Divine Tribunal, Necessary to a Serious Conviction of Gratuitous Justification

I. Sources of Error Surrounding Justification

Though it appears, from the plainest testimonies, that all these things are strictly true, yet we shall not clearly discover how necessary they are till we shall have taken a view of what ought to be the foundation of all this argument.

In the first place, therefore, we should reflect that we are not treating of the righteousness of a human court, but of that of the heavenly tribunal; in order that we may not apply any diminutive standard of our own to estimate the integrity of conduct required to satisfy the Divine justice. But it is wonderful, with what temerity and presumption this is commonly decided; and it is even observable, that no men give us more confident or pompous declamations concerning the righteousness of works than those who are notoriously guilty of open sins or addicted to secret vices. This arises from their never thinking of the righteousness of God, the smallest sense of which would prevent them from treating it with such contempt. And certainly it is exceedingly undervalued, if it be not acknowledged to be so perfect that nothing can be acceptable to it but what is absolutely complete and immaculate, such as it never was, nor ever will be, possible to find in fallen man. It is easy for anyone in the cloisters of the schools to indulge himself in idle speculations on the merit of works to justify men; but when he comes into the presence of God, he must bid farewell to these amusements, for there the business is transacted with seriousness, and no ludicrous logomachy practiced.

To this point, then, must our attention be directed, if we wish to make any useful inquiry concerning true righteousness; how we can answer the celestial Judge when he shall call us to an account. Let us place that Judge before our eyes, not according to the spontaneous imaginations of our minds, but according to the descriptions given of him in the Scripture; which represents him as one whose refulgence eclipses the stars, whose power melts the mountains, whose anger shakes the earth, whose wisdom takes the subtle in their own craftiness, whose purity makes all things appear polluted, whose righteousness even the angels are unable to bear, who acquits not the guilty, whose vengeance, when it is once kindled, penetrates even to the abyss of hell.[1] Let him seat himself, I say, on the tribunal, to examine the actions of men: who will present himself fearless before his throne? "Who shall dwell with the devouring fire?" says the prophet. "Who shall dwell with everlasting burnings? He that walks righteously and speaks uprightly," &c. (Isa. 33:14, 15). Now let him come forward, whoever he is. But this answer causes not one to appear.

For, on the contrary, we hear this fearful speech, "If you, Lord, should mark iniquities, O Lord, who shall stand?" (Psa. 130:3). In truth, all must speedily perish, as it is written in

---

[1] See particularly the Book of Job.

another place, "Shall mortal man be more just than God? Shall a man be more pure than his Maker? Behold, he put no trust in his servants; and his angels he charged with folly; how much less in them that dwell in houses of clay, whose foundation is in the dust, which are crushed before the moth? They are destroyed from morning to evening" (Job 4:17-20). Again: "Behold, he puts no trust in his saints; yea, the heavens are not clean in his sight; how much more abominable and filthy is man, which drinks iniquity like water?" (Job 15:15, 16). I confess that, in the Book of Job, mention is made of a righteousness which is superior to the observance of the law. And it will be of use to remember this distinction; because, though any one could satisfy the law, he could not even then stand the scrutiny of that righteousness which exceeds all comprehension. Therefore, though Job is conscious of his own integrity, yet he is mute with astonishment, when he sees that God could not be pleased even with the sanctity of angels, if he were to enter into a strict examination of their works.

I shall, therefore, now pass over that righteousness to which I have alluded, because it is incomprehensible, and content myself with asserting that we must be worse than stupid if, on an examination of our lives by the rule of the written law, we are not tormented with awful dread in consequence of so many maledictions, which God has designed to arouse us, and among the rest this general one: "Cursed be he that confirms not all the words of this law to do them" (Deut. 27:26). In short, this whole controversy will be uninteresting and useless, unless every one present himself as a criminal before the celestial Judge, and voluntarily prostrate and humble himself in deep solicitude and concerning his absolution.

II. The Deception of False Confidence

To this point, our eyes ought to have been raised that we might learn rather to tremble through fear than to indulge in vain exultation. It is easy, indeed, while the comparison is made only between men, for every man to imagine himself to be possessed of something which others ought not to contemn; but when we ascend to the contemplation of God, that confidence is immediately lost. And the case of our soul with respect to God is similar to that of our body with respect to the visible heavens; for the eye, as long as it is employed in beholding adjacent objects, receives proofs of its own perspicacity; but if it be directed towards the sun, dazzled and confounded with his overpowering brightness, it feels no less debility in beholding him, than strength in the view of inferior objects.

Let us not, then, deceive ourselves with a vain confidence, although we consider ourselves equal or superior to other men. That is nothing to God, to whose decision this cause must be submitted. But if our insolence cannot be restrained by these admonitions, he will reply to us in the language which he addressed to the Pharisees: "You are they which justify yourselves before men; but that which is highly esteemed among men is abomination in the sight of God" (Luke 16:15). Go now, and among men proudly glory in your righteousness, while the God of heaven abominates it. But what is the language of the servants of God who are truly taught by his Spirit? One says, "Enter not into judgment with your servant; for in your sight shall no man living be justified" (Psa. 143:2). And another, though in a sense somewhat different, "How should man be just with God? If he will contend with him, he cannot answer him one of a thousand" (Job 9:2, 3). Here we are plainly informed respecting the righteousness of God that it is such as no human works can satisfy; and such as renders it impossible for us, if accused of a thousand crimes, to exculpate ourselves from one of them. The same idea of his righteousness had very properly been entertained by Paul, that "chosen vessel" (Acts 9:15) of God, when he professed, "I am conscious to myself of nothing; yet am I not hereby justified" (1 Cor. 4:4).

III. Augustine and Bernard on False Confidence

Nor is it only in the sacred Scriptures that such examples are found. All pious writers discover similar sentiments. Thus Augustine says, "The only hope of all the pious, who groan under this burden of corruptible flesh, and amidst the infirmities of this life, is that we have a Mediator, Jesus Christ the righteous; and he is the propitiation for our sins."[2] What is the meaning of this observation? If this is their only hope, where is any confidence in works? For when he asserts this to be the only one, he precludes every other. Bernard also says,

> And in fact where can be found safe and solid rest and security for the weak, but in the wounds of the Savior? There I dwell with the greater security, in proportion to his power to save. The world rages, the body oppresses, the devil lies in wait to destroy. I do not fall, because my foundation is on a firm rock, I have committed heinous sin. My conscience is disturbed, but shall not fall into despair, because I shall recall to remembrance the wounds of the Lord.

---

[2] Augustine, *Against Two Pelagian Letters to Pope Boniface*, vol. 3, c. 5.

From these considerations he afterwards concludes,

> My merit, therefore, is the compassion of the Lord: I am clearly not destitute of merit, as long as he is not destitute of compassions. But if the mercies of the Lord be a multitude of mercies, my merits are likewise equally numerous. Shall I sing of my own righteousness? O Lord, I will remember thy righteousness alone. For it is mine also, since he is made of God righteousness unto me.[3]

Again, in another place: "This is the whole merit of man—to fix all his hope on him who saves the whole man."[4] Likewise in another place, retaining peace to himself, and ascribing the glory to God, he says, "To thee let the glory remain undiminished. It is happy for me, if I have peace. The glory I entirely renounce; lest, if I usurp what is not mine, I lose also that which is offered me."[5] In another place he is still more explicit:

> Why should the Church be solicitous about merits, while it has a stronger and more secure reason for glorying in the designs of God? You need not inquire on account of what merits we hope for blessings, especially when you read in the prophet, "Thus saith the Lord God; I do not this for your sakes, but for mine holy name's sake" [Ezek. 36:22], It suffices with respect to merit, to know that merits are not sufficient; but as it suffices for merit not to presume on merits, so

---

[3] Bernard, *Sermons on the Song of Songs,* serm. 61.
[4] Ibid., serm. 15.
[5] Ibid., serm. 13.

to be destitute of merits is sufficient cause of condemnation.⁶

We must excuse his custom of freely using the word merits for good works. But his ultimate design was to terrify hypocrites who indulge themselves in a licentious course of sin against the grace of God; as he presently declares:

> Happy is the Church which wants neither merits without presumption, nor presumption without merits. It has some ground of presumption, but not merits. It has merits, but in order to deserve, not to presume. Is not the absence of presumption itself a merit? Therefore the Church presumes the more securely, because it does not presume, having ample cause for glorying in the multitude of the Divine mercies.⁷

IV. Examining the Troubled Conscience

This is the real truth. The troubled conscience finds this to be the only asylum of safety, where it can enjoy any tranquility, when it has to do with the Divine justice. For if the stars, which appeared most brilliant during the night, lose their splendor on the rising of the sun, what can we suppose will be the case with the most excellent innocence of man, when compared with the purity of God? For that will be an examination inconceivably severe, which shall penetrate into all the most secret thoughts of the heart, and, as Paul says, "bring to light the hidden things of darkness, and make manifest the counsels of the hearts" (1 Cor. 4:5); which shall constrain the reluctant conscience to confess all those things which have now passed away even from our own

---

⁶ Ibid., serm. 68.
⁷ Ibid.

remembrance. We shall be urged by an accusing devil, who has been privy to all the crimes which he has impelled us to perpetrate.

There the external appearance of good works, which now is the sole object of esteem, will be of no avail; sincerity of heart is all that will be required. Wherefore hypocrisy, not only that by which a man, conscious of his guilt before God, affects ostentation before men, but that also by which every man imposes on himself before God, for we are all prone to self-complacency and adulation; hypocrisy in all its forms will then be overwhelmed with confusion, however it may now be intoxicated with presumption and pride. Persons who never look forward to such a spectacle may, indeed, delightfully and complacently compose for themselves a temporary righteousness, of which they will immediately be stripped at the Divine judgment; just as immense riches, accumulated by us in a dream, vanish as soon as we awake. But they who inquire seriously, and as in the presence of God, respecting the true standard of righteousness, will certainly find that all the actions of men, if estimated according to their intrinsic worth, are utterly defiled and polluted; that what is commonly considered as righteousness is, in the Divine view, nothing but iniquity; that what is accounted integrity is mere pollution; and that what is reputed glory is real ignominy.

V. Facing the Truth of Our Own Miserable Condition

From this contemplation of the Divine perfection, let us not be unwilling to descend to take a view of ourselves without adulation or blind self-love. For it is not to be wondered at, if we are so extremely blind in this respect, since not one of us is sufficiently cautious of that pestilent self-indulgence, which the

Consideration of the Divine Tribunal

Scripture declares to be naturally inherent in us all. "Every way of man," says Solomon, "is right in his own eyes" (Prov. 21:2). Again: "All the ways of a man are clean in his own eyes" (Prov. 16:2). But what follows from this? Is he absolved from guilt by this delusion? Not at all; but, as is immediately added, "the Lord weighs the spirits;" that is, while men are congratulating themselves on account of the external mask of righteousness which they wear, the Lord is at the same time weighing in his own balance the latent impurity of their hearts.

Since we are so far from deriving any advantage, therefore, from such blandishments, let us not voluntarily delude ourselves to our own perdition. That we may examine ourselves properly, it is necessary for us to summon our conscience to the tribunal of God. For we have the greatest need of his light in order to detect the recesses of our depravity, which otherwise are too deeply concealed. For then only shall we clearly perceive the force of this language: "How can man be justified with God—man, who is" corruption and "a worm, abominable and filthy, and who drinks iniquity like water" (Job 15:16; 25:4, 6)? "Who can bring a clean thing out of an unclean? Not one" (Job 14:4). Then also we shall experience what Job said concerning himself: "If I justify myself, mine own mouth shall condemn me; if I say I am perfect, it shall also prove me perverse" (Job 9:20). For the complaint, which the prophet formerly made respecting Israel, "All we like sheep have gone astray; we have turned everyone to his own way" (Isa. 53:6); is applicable not only to one period of time, but to all ages. For he there comprehends all to whom the grace of redemption was to extend; and the rigor of this examination ought to proceed till it shall have filled us with complete consternation, and thus prepared us to receive the grace of Christ. For he is deceived who supposes himself capable of this enjoyment without having first been truly humbled. It is a well-known observation that "God resists the proud, and gives grace to the humble" (1 Pet. 5:5).

VI. Attaining to Humility by Apprehending Christ by Faith
But what means have we of humbling ourselves, except by submitting, all poor and destitute, to the Divine mercy? For I do not call it humility if we suppose that we have anything left. And hitherto they have taught a pernicious hypocrisy, who have connected these two maxims—that we should entertain humble thoughts of ourselves before God, and that we should attach some dignity to our own righteousness. For if we address to God a confession which is contrary to our real sentiments, we are guilty of telling him an impudent falsehood; but we cannot think of ourselves as we ought to think, without utterly despising everything that may be supposed an excellence in us.

When we hear, therefore, from the Psalmist that "God will save the afflicted people, but will bring down high looks" (Psa. 18:27), let us consider, first, that there is no way of salvation till we have laid aside all pride, and attained sincere humility; secondly, that this humility is not a species of modesty, consisting in conceding to God a small portion of what we might justly claim, as they are called humble among men, who neither haughtily exalt themselves nor behave with insolence to others, while they nevertheless entertain some consciousness of excellence. This humility is the unfeigned submission of a mind overwhelmed with a weighty sense of its own misery and poverty; for such is the uniform description of it in the word of God.

When the Lord speaks thus in Zephaniah, "I will take away out of the midst of you them that rejoice in your pride; I will also leave in the midst of you an afflicted and poor people, and they shall trust in the name of the Lord" (Zeph. 3:11, 12); does he not clearly show who are truly humble? even such as are afflicted with a knowledge of their own poverty. On the contrary, he describes the proud as persons "rejoicing," because this is the usual consequence of prosperity. But to the humble, whom he intends to save, he leaves nothing but that "they trust in the name of the Lord."

Thus also in Isaiah, "To this man will I look, even to him that is poor and of a contrite spirit, and trembles at my word" (Isa. 66:2). Again: "Thus says the high and lofty One that inhabits eternity, whose name is Holy; 'I dwell in the high and holy place with him also that is of a contrite and humble spirit, to revive the spirit of the humble, and to revive the heart of the contrite ones'" (Isa. 57:15). By the contrition so frequently mentioned, we must understand a wounded heart, which prevents a man from rising when humbled in the dust. With such contrition must our heart be wounded, if we desire, according to the declaration of the Lord, to be exalted with the humble. If this be not the case, we shall be abased by the powerful hand of God to our shame and disgrace (Matt. 23:12; Luke 14:11; 18:14).

VII. The Parable of the Publican

And, not content with mere precepts, our excellent Master in a parable, as in a picture, has presented us with an example of genuine humility. For he introduces a publican who, "standing afar off, would not lift up so much as his eyes unto heaven, but smote upon his breast, saying, 'God be merciful to me a sinner'" (Luke 18:13). We must not conclude these circumstances—his not presuming to look upwards, standing

JUSTIFICATION BY FAITH

afar off, smiting upon his breast, and confessing himself a sinner—to be marks of feigned modesty. We may be certain that they were sincere evidences of the disposition of his heart. To him our Lord opposes a Pharisee who said, "God, I thank you that I am not as other men are, extortioners, unjust, adulterers, or even as this publican. I fast twice in the week, I give tithes of all that I possess." He openly confesses the righteousness which he has, to be the gift of God; but because he confides in his being righteous, he departs from the presence of God unacceptable and hateful to him. The publican, acknowledging his iniquity, is justified.

Hence we may see how very pleasing our humiliation is in the sight of God; so that the heart is not open for the reception of his mercy unless it be divested of all idea of its own dignity. When this notion has occupied the mind, it precludes the admission of Divine mercy. That no one might have any doubt of this, Christ was sent by his Father into the world with a commission, "to preach good tidings unto the meek; to bind up the broken-hearted; to proclaim liberty to the captives, and the opening of the prison to them that are bound; to comfort all that mourn; to give unto them beauty for ashes, the oil of joy for mourning, the garment of praise for the spirit of heaviness" (Isa. 61:1-3). In pursuance of this commission, he invites to a participation of his benefits none but those who "labor and are heavy laden" (Matt. 11:28). And in another place he says, "I am not come to call the righteous, but sinners to repentance" (Matt. 9:13).

VIII. Rejecting Self-Sufficiency

Therefore, if we would obey the call of Christ, let us dismiss all arrogance and carelessness from our minds. The former arises from a foolish persuasion of our own righteousness when a man supposes himself to be possessed of anything, the merit of which can recommend him to God; the latter may exist without any consideration of works. For multitudes of sinners, inebriated with criminal pleasures, and forgetful of the Divine judgment, are in a state, as it were, of lethargic insensibility, so that they never aspire after the mercy which is offered to them.

But it is equally necessary for us to shake off such stupidity, and to reject all confidence in ourselves, in order that, being freed from every encumbrance, we may hasten to Christ all destitute and hungry, to be filled with his blessings. For we shall never have sufficient confidence in him, unless we entirely lose all confidence in ourselves; we shall never find sufficient encouragement in him, unless we are previously dejected in ourselves; we shall never enjoy sufficient consolation in him, unless we are utterly disconsolate in ourselves.

We are prepared, therefore, to seek and obtain the grace of God, discarding at the same time all confidence in ourselves, and relying solely on the assurance of his mercy, "when," as Augustine says, "forgetting our own merits, we embrace the free gifts of Christ; because, if he sought merits in us, we should not come to his free gifts."[8] With him Bernard fully agrees, when he compares proud men that arrogate ever so little to their own merits, to unfaithful servants, because they unjustly claim the praise of the grace which passes through them; just as though a wall should say that it produces the sunbeams which it receives through a window.[9]

But not to dwell any longer on this, we may lay it down as a brief, but general and certain maxim, that he is prepared for a

---

[8] Augustine, *Sermon on the Apostolic Word*, serm. 8.
[9] Bernard, *Sermons on the Song of Songs*, serm. 13.

participation of the benefits of Divine mercy, who has wholly divested himself, I will not say of his righteousness, which is a mere nullity, but of the vain and airy phantom of righteousness; for as far as any man is satisfied with himself, so far he raises an impediment to the exercise of the grace of God.

3

Two Things Necessary to Be Observed in Gratuitous Justification

I. The Glory and Justice of God

Here are two things to which we must always be particularly attentive: to maintain the glory of the Lord unimpaired and undiminished, and to preserve in our own consciences a placid composure and serene tranquility with regard to the Divine judgment. We see how frequently and solicitously the Scripture exhorts us to render ascriptions of praise to God alone, when it treats of justification. And, indeed, the apostle assures us that the design of the Lord in conferring righteousness upon us in Christ is to manifest his own righteousness. The nature of that manifestation he immediately subjoins: it is, "that he might be just, and the justifier of him which believes in Jesus" (Rom. 3:26). The righteousness of God, we see, is not sufficiently illustrious, unless he alone be esteemed righteous, and communicate the grace of justification to the unworthy. For this reason it is his will "that every mouth be stopped, and all the world become guilty before him" (Rom. 3:19); because, as long as man has anything to allege in his own defense, it detracts something from the glory of God. Thus in Ezekiel he teaches us how greatly we glorify his name by an acknowledgment of our iniquity:

> You shall remember your ways (he says), and all your doings, wherein you have been defiled; and you shall loathe yourselves in your own sight for all your evils that you have committed. And you shall know that I am the Lord, when I have wrought with you for my name's sake, not according to your wicked ways, nor according to your corrupt doings (Ezek. 20:43-44).

If these things are contained in the true knowledge of God that, humbled with a consciousness of our iniquity, we should consider him as indulging us with blessings of which we are unworthy, why do we attempt, to our own serious injury, to pilfer the smallest particle of the praise due to his gratuitous goodness? Thus also when Jeremiah proclaims, "Let not the wise man glory in his wisdom, neither let the mighty man glory in his might, let not the rich man glory in his riches; but let him that glories glory in the Lord" (Jer. 9:23-24); does he not suggest that the glory of God sustains some diminution, if any man glory in himself? To this use these words are clearly applied by Paul, when he states, that all the branches of our salvation are deposited with Christ, that we may not glory except in the Lord (1 Cor. 1:29-31). For he intimates that they who suppose themselves to have even the least ground for glorying in themselves are guilty of rebelling against God and obscuring his glory.

II. The Error of Those Who Would Glory in Themselves

The truth, then, is that we never truly glory in him till we have entirely renounced all glory of our own. On the converse, this

Two Things Necessary

may be admitted as an axiom universally true, that they who glory in themselves, glory in opposition to God. For Paul is of opinion that the world is not "subject to the judgment of God," till men are deprived of all foundation for glorying (Rom. 3:19). Therefore Isaiah, when he announces that "in the Lord shall all the seed of Israel be justified," adds also, "and shall glory;" as though he had said that the end of God in justifying the elect was that they might glory in himself, and in no other. But how we should glory in the Lord, he had stated in the preceding verse, "Surely, shall one say, in the Lord have I righteousness and strength." Let us observe that what is required is not a simple confession, but a confession confirmed by an oath; that we may not suppose any fictitious pretense of humility to be sufficient (Isa. 45:23-25). Here let no one plead that he does not glory at all, when without arrogance he recognizes his own righteousness; for such an opinion cannot exist without generating confidence, nor confidence without being attended with glorying.

Let us remember, therefore, in the whole controversy concerning righteousness, that this end must be kept in view, that all the praise of it may remain perfect and undiminished with the Lord; because, according to the apostle's testimony, he has bestowed his grace on us in order "to declare his righteousness; that he might be just, and the justifier of him which believes in Jesus" (Rom. 3:26). Wherefore, in another place, after having declared that the Lord has conferred salvation on us in order to display "the praise of the glory of his grace" (Eph. 1:6), repeating, as it were, the same sentiment, he adds, "By grace are you saved through faith; and that not of yourselves; it is the gift of God; not of works, lest any man should boast" (Eph. 2:8). And when Peter admonishes us that we are called to the hope of salvation, "that we should show forth the praises (or virtues) of him who has called us out of darkness into his marvelous light" (1 Pet. 2:9), he evidently means that the praises of God alone should resound in the ears of believers, so as to impose total silence on all the presumption of the flesh. The conclusion of the whole is that man cannot without sacrilege arrogate to himself the least particle of righteousness, because it is so much detracted and diminished from the glory of the righteousness of God.

III. Obtaining a Clear Conscience

Now, if we inquire by what means the conscience can obtain peace before God, we shall find no other than our reception of gratuitous righteousness from his free gift. Let us always remember the inquiry of Solomon—"Who can say, I have made my heart clean, I am pure from my sin" (Prov. 20:9)? It is certain that there is no man who is not covered with infinite pollution. Let a man of the most perfect character, then, retire into his own conscience, and enter into a scrutiny of his actions, and what will be the result? Will he feel a high degree of satisfaction, as though there were the most entire agreement between God and him? Or will he not rather be lacerated with terrible agonies on perceiving in himself such ample cause for condemnation, if he be judged according to his works? If the conscience reflect on God, it must either enjoy a solid peace with his judgment, or be surrounded with the terrors of hell.

We gain nothing, therefore, in our discussions of this point, unless we establish a righteousness, the stability of which will support our souls under the scrutiny of the Divine judgment. When our souls shall possess what will enable them to appear with boldness in the presence of God, and to await and receive his judgment without any fear, then, and not before, we may be assured that we have found a righteousness which truly deserves the name. It is not without reason, therefore, that this subject is so largely insisted on by the apostle, whose words I prefer to my own: "For if they which are of the law be heirs, faith is made void, and the promise is made of none effect" (Rom. 4:14). He first infers that faith is annulled and superseded if the promise of righteousness respect the merit of our works, or depend on our observance of the law. For no man could ever securely rely on it, since he never would be able to determine with certainty for himself that he had fulfilled the law, as in fact no man ever does completely satisfy it by any works of his own. Not to seek far for testimonies of this fact, every individual may be his own witness of it, who will enter unprejudiced into an examination of himself. And hence it appears in what deep and dark recesses hypocrisy buries the minds of men, while they indulge themselves in such great security, and hesitate not to oppose their self-adulation to the judgment of God, as though they would stop the proceedings of his tribunal.

But believers, who sincerely examine themselves, are troubled and distressed with a solicitude of a very different nature. The minds of men universally, therefore, ought to feel first hesitation, and then despair, while considering, every one for himself, the magnitude of the debt with which they are still oppressed, and their immense distance from the conditions prescribed to them. Behold their confidence already broken and extinguished; for to confide is not to fluctuate, to vary, to be hurried hither and thither, to hesitate, to be kept in suspense, to stagger, and finally to despair; but it is to strengthen the mind with content, certainty, and solid security, and to have somewhat upon which to stand and to rest.

IV. The Promise of God Confirmed by Faith

He adds likewise another consideration that the promise would be void and of none effect. For if the fulfilment of it depend on our merit, when shall we have made such a progress as to deserve the favor of God? Besides, this second argument is a consequence of the former, since the promise will be fulfilled to those alone who shall exercise faith in it. Therefore, if faith be wanting, the promise will retain no force. "Therefore the inheritance is of faith that it might be by grace; to the end the promise might be sure to all the seed" (Rom. 4:16). For it is abundantly confirmed when it depends solely on the Divine mercy, because mercy and truth are connected by an indissoluble bond, and whatever God mercifully promises, he also faithfully performs.

Thus David, before he implores salvation for himself according to the word of God, first represents it as originating in his mercy: "According to your word unto your servant, let your tender mercies come unto me, that I may live" (Psa. 119:76, 77). And for this there is sufficient reason, since God has no other inducement to promise than what arises from his mere mercy. Here, then, we must place and, as it were, deeply fix all our hopes without regarding our own works, or seeking any assistance from them. Nor must it be supposed that we are advancing a new doctrine, for the same conduct is recommended by Augustine. "Christ," says he, "will reign in his servants forever. God has promised this, God has said it; if that be insufficient, God has sworn it. Since the promise, therefore, is established, not according to our merits, but according to his mercy, no man ought to speak with anxiety of that which he cannot doubt."[1] Bernard also says,

> The disciples of Christ asked, "Who can be saved?" He replied, "With men this is impossible, but not with God." This is all our confidence, this our only consolation, this the whole foundation of our hope. But certain of the possibility, what think we of his will? Who knows whether he deserve love or hatred? [Eccl. 9:1] Who has known the mind of the Lord, or who has been his counselor? [1 Cor. 2:16] Here, now, we evidently need faith to help us, and his truth to assist us; that what is concealed from us in the heart of the Father, may be revealed by the Spirit, and that the testimony of the Spirit may persuade our hearts that we are sons of God; that he may persuade us by calling and justifying us freely by faith; in which there is, as it were, an intermediate passage eternal predestination to future glory.[2]

Let us draw the following brief conclusion: The Scripture declares that the promises of God have no efficacy unless they be embraced by the conscience with a steady confidence; and whenever there is any doubt or uncertainty, it pronounces them to be made void. Again, it asserts that they have no stability if they depend on our works. Either, therefore, we must be forever destitute of righteousness, or our works must not come into consideration, but the ground must be occupied by faith alone, whose nature it is to harken the ears and shut the eyes; that is, to be intent only on the promise, and to avert the thoughts from all human dignity or merit. Thus is accomplished that remarkable

---

[1] Augustine, *Expositions on the Psalms,* 88, tract. 50.
[2] Bernard, *Sermons,* in 5, dedica, templi.

prophecy of Zechariah, "I will remove the iniquity of that land in one day. In that day, says the Lord of hosts, shall you call every man his neighbor under the vine and under the fig-tree" (Zech. 3:9, 10); in which the prophet suggests that believers enjoy no true peace till after they obtained the remission of their sins. For this analogy must be observed in the prophets, that when they treat of the kingdom of Christ, they exhibit the external bounties of God as figures of spiritual blessings. Wherefore also Christ is denominated "the Prince of peace," and "our Peace" (Isa. 9:6; cf. Eph. 2:14); because he calms all the agitations of the conscience. If we inquire, by what means; we must come to the sacrifice by which God is appeased. For no man will ever lose his fears who shall not be assured that God is propitiated solely by that atonement which Christ has made by sustaining his wrath. In short, we must seek for peace only in the terrors of Christ our Redeemer.

V. Paul's Testimony Against Sophism

But why do I use such an obscure testimony? Paul invariably denies that peace or tranquility can be enjoyed in the conscience without a certainty that we are justified by faith (Rom. 5:1). And he also declares whence that certainty proceeds; it is "because the love of God is shed abroad in our hearts by the Holy Ghost" (Rom. 5:5); as though he had said that our consciences can never be satisfied without a certain persuasion of our acceptance with God. Hence he exclaims in the name of all believers, "Who shall separate us from the love of God which is in Christ" (Rom. 8:35ff.)? For till we have reached that port of safety, we shall tremble with alarm at every slightest breeze; but while God shall manifest himself as our Shepherd, we shall fear no evil even in the valley of the shadow of death (Psa. 23:4).

Two Things Necessary

Whoever they are, therefore, who pretend that we are justified by faith because, being regenerated, we are righteous by living a spiritual life, they have never tasted the sweetness of grace, so as to have confidence that God would be propitious to them. Whence also it follows that they know no more of the method of praying aright than the Turks or any other profane nations. For according to the testimony of Paul, faith is not genuine unless it dictate and suggest that most delightful name of Father, and unless it open our mouth freely to cry, "Abba, Father" (Gal. 4:6); which he in another place expresses still more clearly: "In Christ we have boldness and access with confidence by the faith of him" (Eph. 3:12). This certainly arises not from the gift of regeneration; which, being always imperfect in the present state, contains in itself abundant occasion of doubting.

Wherefore it is necessary to come to this remedy; that believers should conclude that they cannot hope for an inheritance in the kingdom of heaven on any other foundation, but because, being engrafted into the body of Christ, they are gratuitously accounted righteous. For with respect to justification, faith is a thing merely passive, bringing nothing of our own to conciliate the favor of God, but receiving what we need from Christ.

4

The Commencement and Continual Progress of Justification

I. Four Classes of Unrighteous Men

For the further elucidation of this subject, let us examine what kind of righteousness can be found in men during the whole course of their lives. Let us divide them into four classes. For either (1) they are destitute of the knowledge of God, and immerged in idolatry; or, (2) having been initiated by the sacraments, they lead impure lives, denying God in their actions, while they confess him with their lips, and belong to Christ only in name; or (3) they are hypocrites, concealing the iniquity of their hearts with vain disguises; or, (4) being regenerated by the Spirit of God, they devote themselves to true holiness.

In the first of these classes, judged of according to their natural characters, from the crown of the head to the sole of the foot there will not be found a single spark of goodness; unless we mean to charge the Scripture with falsehood in these representations which it gives of all the sons of Adam—that "the heart is deceitful above all things, and desperately wicked" (Jer. 17:9); that "every imagination of man's heart is evil from his youth" (Gen. 6:5; 8:21); that "the thoughts of man are vanity; that there is no fear of God before his eyes" (Psa. 94:11;

36:1); that "there is none that understands, none that seeks after God" (Psa. 14:1-3; cf. Rom. 3:11); in a word, "that he is flesh" (Gen. 6:3), a term expressive of all those works which are enumerated by Paul—"adultery, fornication, uncleanness, lasciviousness, idolatry, witchcraft, hatred, variance, emulations, wrath, strife, seditions, heresies, envyings, murders" (Gal. 5:19ff.), and every impurity and abomination that can be conceived. This is the dignity in the confidence of which they must glory. But if any among them discover that integrity in their conduct which among men has some appearance of sanctity, yet since we know that God regards not external splendor, we must penetrate to the secret springs of these actions, if we wish them to avail anything to justification.

We must narrowly examine, I say, from what disposition of heart these works proceed. Though a most extensive field of observation is now before us, yet since the subject may be dispatched in very few words, I shall be as compendious as possible.

II. Various Differences Between Men

In the first place, I do not deny that whatever excellences appear in unbelievers, they are the gifts of God. I am not so at variance with the common opinion of mankind as to contend that there is no difference between the justice, moderation, and equity of Titus or Trajan, and the rage, intemperance, and cruelty of Caligula, or Nero, or Domitian; between the obscenities of Tiberius and the continence of Vespasian; and, not to dwell on particular virtues or vices, between the observance and the contempt of moral obligation and positive laws. For so great is the difference between just and unjust, that it is visible even in the lifeless image of it. For what order will be left in the world if these opposites be confounded together?

Such a distinction as this, therefore, between virtuous and vicious actions has not only been engraven by the Lord in the heart of every man, but has also been frequently confirmed by his providential dispensations. We see how he confers many blessings of the present life on those who practice virtue among men. Not that this external resemblance of virtue merits the least favor from him; but he is pleased to discover his great esteem of true righteousness, by not permitting that which is external and hypocritical to remain without a temporal reward. Whence it follows, as we have just acknowledged, that these virtues, whatever they may be, or rather images of virtues, are the gifts of God; since there is nothing in any respect laudable which does not proceed from him.

III. The Inherent Corruption of Human Virtue

Nevertheless, the observation of Augustine is strictly true—that all who are strangers to the religion of the one true God, however they may be esteemed worthy of admiration for their reputed virtue, not only merit no reward, but are rather deserving of punishment because they contaminate the pure gifts of God with the pollution of their own hearts. For though they are instruments used by God for the preservation of human society, by the exercise of justice, continence, friendship, temperance, fortitude, and prudence, yet they perform these good works of God very improperly; being restrained from the commission of evil, not by a sincere attachment to true virtue, but either by mere ambition, or by self-love, or by some other irregular disposition.

These actions, therefore, being corrupted in their very source by the impurity of their hearts, are no more entitled to be classed among virtues than those vices which commonly deceive mankind by their affinity and similitude to virtues. Besides, when we remember that the end of what is right is always to serve God, whatever is directed to any other end, can have no claim to that appellation. Therefore, since they regard not the end prescribed by Divine wisdom, though an act performed by them be externally and apparently good, yet being directed to a wrong end, it becomes sin. He concludes, therefore, that all the Fabricii, Scipios, and Catos, in all their celebrated actions, were guilty of sin, inasmuch as, being destitute of the light of faith, they did not direct those actions to that end to which they ought to have directed them; that consequently they had no genuine righteousness; because moral duties are estimated not by external actions, but by the ends for which such actions are designed.

IV. Life Found Only in Christ

Besides, if there be any truth in the assertion of John that "he that has not the Son of God, has not life" (1 John 5:12); they who have no interest in Christ, whatever be their characters, their actions, or their endeavors, are constantly advancing, through the whole course of their lives, towards destruction and the sentence of eternal death. On this argument is founded the following observation of Augustine: "Our religion discriminates between the righteous and the unrighteous, not by the law of works, but by that of faith, without which works apparently good are perverted into sins."[1]

---

[1] Augustine, *Against Two Pelagian Letters to Pope Boniface,* vol. 3, c. 5.

Wherefore the same writer, in another place, strikingly compares the exertions of such men to a deviation in a race from the prescribed course. For the more vigorously any one runs out of the way, he recedes so much the further from the goal, and becomes so much the more unfortunate. Wherefore he contends, that it is better to halt in the way, than to run out of the way.

Finally, it is evident that they are evil trees, since without a participation of Christ there is no sanctification. They may produce fruits fair and beautiful to the eye, and even sweet to the taste, but never any that are good. Hence we clearly perceive that all the thoughts, meditations, and actions of man antecedent to a reconciliation to God by faith are accursed, and not only of no avail to justification, but certainly deserving of condemnation. But why do we dispute concerning it as a dubious point, when it is already proved by the testimony of the apostle, that "without faith it is impossible to please God" (Heb. 11:6)?

V. The Natural Condition of All Men

But the proof will be still clearer, if the grace of God be directly opposed to the natural condition of man. The Scripture invariably proclaims that God finds nothing in men which can incite him to bless them, but that he prevents them by his gratuitous goodness. For what can a dead man do to recover life? But when God illuminates us with the knowledge of himself, he is said to raise us from death, and to make us new creatures (John 5:25). For under this character we find the Divine goodness towards us frequently celebrated, especially by the apostle. "God," says he, "who is rich in mercy, for his great love wherewith he loved us, even when we were dead in sins, has quickened us together with Christ," &c. (Eph. 2:4, 5). In another place, when, under the type of Abraham, he treats of the general calling of believers, he says, "[It is] God, who quickens the dead, and calls those things which be not as though they were" (Rom. 4:17). If we are nothing, what can we do?

Wherefore God forcibly represses this presumption in the Book of Job, in the following words: "Who has prevented me, that I should repay him? Whatsoever is under the whole heaven is mine" (Job 41:11). Paul, explaining this passage, concludes from it that we ought not to suppose we bring anything to the Lord but ignominious indigence and emptiness (Rom. 11:35). Wherefore, in the passage cited above, in order to prove that we attain to the hope of salvation, not by works, but solely by the grace of God, he alleges that "we are his workmanship, created in Christ Jesus unto good works, which God has before ordained that we should walk in them" (Eph. 2:10). As though he would say, Who of us can boast that he has influenced God by his righteousness, since our first power to do well proceeds from regeneration? For, according to the constitution of our nature, oil might be extracted from a stone sooner than we could perform a good work. It is wonderful, indeed, that man, condemned to such ignominy, dares to pretend to have anything left.

Let us confess, therefore, with that eminent servant of the Lord, that "God has saved us, and called us with a holy calling, not according to our works, but according to his own purpose and grace" (2 Tim. 1:9); and that "the kindness and love of God our Savior towards man appeared," because "not by works of righteousness which we have done, but according to his mercy he saved us; that being justified by his grace, we should be made heirs of eternal life" (Titus 3:4, 5, 7). By this confession we divest man of all righteousness, even to the smallest particle, till through mere mercy he has been regenerated to the hope of eternal life. For if a righteousness of works contributed anything to our justification, we are not truly said to be "justified by grace." The apostle, when he asserted justification to be by grace, had certainly not forgotten his argument in another place, that "if it be of works, then it is no more grace" (Rom. 11:6). And what else does our Lord intend when he declares, "I am not come to call the righteous, but sinners" (Matt. 9:13)? If sinners only are admitted, why do we seek to enter by a counterfeit righteousness?

VI. Confounding Human Works with Christ's Redemption
The same thought frequently recurs to me, that I am in danger of injuring the mercy of God by laboring with so much anxiety in the defense of this doctrine, as though it were doubtful or obscure. But such being our malignity that, unless it be most powerfully subdued, it never allows to God that which belongs to him, I am constrained to dwell a little longer upon it. But as the Scripture is sufficiently perspicuous on this subject, I shall use its language in preference to my own.

Isaiah, after having described the universal ruin of mankind, properly subjoins the method of recovery. "The Lord saw it, and it displeased him that there was no judgment. And he saw that there was no man, and wondered that there was no intercessor: therefore his own arm brought salvation unto him; and his righteousness it sustained him" (Isa. 59:15, 16). Where are our righteousnesses, if it be true, as the prophet says, that no one assists the Lord in procuring his salvation? So another prophet introduces the Lord speaking of the reconciliation of sinners to himself, saying, "I will betroth you unto me forever, in righteousness, and in judgment, and in loving-kindness, and in mercies. I will have mercy upon her that had not obtained mercy" (Hos. 2:19, 23). If this covenant, which is evidently our first union with God, depend on his mercy, there remains no foundation for our righteousness. And I should really wish to be informed by those who pretend that man advances to meet God with some righteousness of works, whether there be any righteousness at all, but that which is accepted by God. If it be madness to entertain such a thought, what that is acceptable to God can proceed from his enemies, who, with all their actions, are the objects of his complete abhorrence? And that we are all the inveterate and avowed enemies of our God, till we are justified and received into his friendship, is an undeniable truth (Rom. 5:6, 10; cf. Col. 1:21). If justification be the principle from which love originates, what righteousnesses of works can precede it? To destroy that pestilent arrogance, therefore, John carefully apprizes us that "we did not first love him" (1 John 4:10).

And the Lord had by his prophet long before taught the same truth: "I will love them freely," says he, "for mine anger is turned away" (Hos. 14:4). If his love was spontaneously inclined towards us, it certainly is not excited by works. But the ignorant mass of mankind have only this notion of it—that no man has merited that Christ should effect our redemption; but that towards obtaining the possession of redemption, we derive some assistance from our own works. But however we may have been redeemed by Christ, yet till we are introduced into communion with him by the calling of the Father, we are both heirs of darkness and death, and enemies to God. For Paul teaches that we are not purified and washed from our pollutions by the blood of Christ till the Spirit effects that purification within us (1 Cor. 6:11). This is the same that Peter intends, when he declares that the "sanctification of the Spirit" is effectual "unto obedience, and sprinkling of the blood of Jesus Christ" (1 Pet. 1:2). If we are sprinkled by the Spirit with the blood of Christ for purification, we must not imagine that before this ablution we are in any other state than that of sinners destitute of Christ. We may be certain, therefore, that the commencement of our salvation is, as it were, a resurrection from death to life; because when "on the behalf of Christ it is given to us to believe on him" (Phil. 1:29), we then begin to experience a transition from death to life.

VII. Approaching Hypocrites and False Professors
The same reasoning may be applied to the second and third classes of men in the division stated above. For the impurity of the conscience proves that they are neither of them yet regenerated by the Spirit of God; and their unregeneracy betrays also their want of faith: whence it appears that they are not yet reconciled to God or justified in his sight, since these blessings are only attained by faith. What can be performed by sinners alienated from God that is not execrable in his view? Yet all the impious, and especially hypocrites, are inflated with this foolish confidence. Though they know that their heart is full of impurity, yet if they perform any specious actions, they esteem them too good to be despised by God.

Hence that pernicious error that, though convicted of a polluted and impious heart, they cannot be brought to confess themselves destitute of righteousness; but while they acknowledge themselves to be unrighteous, because it cannot be denied, they still arrogate to themselves some degree of righteousness. This vanity the Lord excellently refutes by the prophet. "Ask now," says he, "the priests, saying, 'If one bear holy flesh in the skirt of his garment, and with his skirt do touch bread, or any meat, shall it be holy?' And the priests answered and said, 'No.' Then said Haggai, 'If one that is unclean by a dead body touch any of these, shall it be unclean?' And the priests answered and said, 'It shall be unclean.' Then answered Haggai and said, 'So is this people, and so is this nation before me,' says the Lord; and so is every work of their hands; and that which they offer there is unclean" (Hag. 2:11-14). I wish that this passage might either obtain full credit with us, or be deeply impressed on our memory. For there is no one, however flagitious his whole life may be, who can suffer himself to be persuaded of what the Lord here plainly declares. The greatest sinner, as soon as he has performed two or three duties of the law, doubts not but they are accepted of him for righteousness; but the Lord positively denies that any sanctification is acquired by such actions, unless the heart be previously well purified; and not content with this, he asserts that all the works of sinners are contaminated by the impurity of their hearts.

Let the name of righteousness, then, no longer be given to these works which are condemned for their pollution by the lips of God. And by what a fine similitude does he demonstrate this! For it might have been objected that what the Lord had enjoined was inviolably holy. But he shows, on the contrary, that it is not to be wondered at, if those things which are sanctified by the law of the Lord, are defiled by the pollution of the wicked; since an unclean hand cannot touch anything that has been consecrated without profaning it.

VIII. Gleanings from Augustine and Gregory

He excellently pursues the same argument also in Isaiah: "Bring no more vain oblations; incense is an abomination unto me; your new moons and your appointed feasts my soul hates; they are a trouble unto me; I am weary to bear them. When you spread forth your hands, I will hide mine eyes from you; yea, when you make many prayers, I will not hear: your hands are full of blood. Wash you, make you clean; put away the evil of your doings" (Isa. 1:13, 16). What is the reason that the Lord is so displeased at an obedience to his law? But, in fact, he here rejects nothing that arises from the genuine observance of the law; the beginning of which, he everywhere teaches is an unfeigned fear of his name (Deut. 4:6; cf. Psa. 111:10; Prov. 1:7; 9:10). If that be wanting, all the oblations made to him are not merely trifles, but nauseous and abominable pollutions. Let hypocrites go now and, retaining depravity concealed in their hearts, endeavor by their works to merit the favor of God. But by such means they will add provocation to provocation; for "the sacrifice of the wicked is an abomination to the Lord; but the prayer of the upright" alone "is his delight" (Prov. 15:8).

We lay it down, therefore, as an undoubted truth, which ought to be well known to such as are but moderately versed in the Scriptures, that even the most splendid works of men not yet truly sanctified, are so far from righteousness in the Divine view, that they are accounted sins. And therefore they have strictly adhered to the truth, who have maintained that the works of a man do not conciliate God's favor to his person; but, on the contrary, that works are never acceptable to God, unless the person who performs them has previously found favor in his sight.[2] And this order, to which the Scripture directs us, is religiously to be observed. Moses relates, that "The Lord had respect unto Abel and to his offering" (Gen. 4:4). Does he not

---

[2] See Augustine, *Repentance*; and Gregory, quoted in Lombard, *Sentences*, vol. 3, quest. 7.

plainly indicate that the Lord is propitious to men before he regards their works? Wherefore the purification of the heart is a necessary prerequisite, in order that, the works which we perform may be favorably received by God; for the declaration of Jeremiah is always in force, that the "eyes of the Lord are upon the truth" (Jer. 5:3). And the Holy Spirit has asserted by the mouth of Peter that it is "by faith" alone that the "heart" is "purified" (Acts 15:9), which proves that the first foundation is laid in a true and living faith.

IX. The Sinful Challenges of the Regenerate

Let us now examine what degree of righteousness is possessed by those whom we have ranked in the fourth class. We admit that when God, by the interposition of the righteousness of Christ, reconciles us to himself, and having granted us the free remission of our sins, esteems us as righteous persons, to this mercy he adds also another blessing. For he dwells in us by his Holy Spirit, by whose power our carnal desires are daily more and more mortified, and we are sanctified, that is, consecrated to the Lord unto real purity of life, having our hearts molded to obey his law, so that it is our prevailing inclination to submit to his will, and to promote his glory alone by all possible means.

But even while, under the guidance of the Holy Spirit, we are walking in the ways of the Lord,—that we may not forget ourselves, and be filled with pride, we feel such remains of imperfection, as afford us abundant cause for humility. The Scripture declares that "there is not a just man upon earth that does good and sins not" (Eccl. 7:20). What kind of righteousness, then, will even believers obtain from their own works?

In the first place, I assert that the best of their performances are tarnished and corrupted by some carnal impurity and debased by a mixture of some alloy. Let any holy servant of God select from his whole life that which he shall conceive to have been the best of all his actions, and let him examine it with attention on every side; he will undoubtedly discover in it some taint of the corruption of the flesh, since our alacrity to good actions is never what it ought to be, but our course is retarded by great debility. Though we perceive that the blemishes which deform the works of the saints are not difficult to be discovered, yet suppose we admit them to be very diminutive spots, will they not be at all offensive in the sight of God, in which even the stars are not pure? We have now ascertained that there is not a single action performed by the saints, which, if judged according to its intrinsic merit, does not justly deserve to be rewarded with shame.

X. Works Righteousness Cannot Justify

In the next place, even though it were possible for us to perform any works completely pure and perfect, yet one sin is sufficient to extinguish and annihilate all remembrance of antecedent righteousness, as is declared by the prophet (Ezek. 18:24). With him James also agrees: "Whosoever shall offend," says he, "in one point, he is guilty of all" (Jas. 2:10). Now, since this mortal life is never pure or free from sin, whatever righteousness we might acquire being perpetually corrupted, overpowered, and destroyed by subsequent sins, it would neither be admitted in the sight of God, nor be imputed to us for righteousness.

Lastly, in considering the righteousness of works, we should regard, not any action commanded in the law, but the commandment itself. Therefore, if we seek righteousness by the law, it is in vain for us to perform two or three works; a perpetual observance of the law is indispensably necessary. Wherefore God does not impute to us for righteousness that remission of sins, of which we have spoken, once only (as some foolishly imagine), in order that, having obtained pardon for our past lives, we may afterwards seek righteousness by the law; which would be only sporting with us, and deluding us by a fallacious hope. For since perfection is unattainable by us, as long as we are in this mortal body, and the law denounces death and judgment on all whose works are not completely and universally righteous, it will always have matter of accusation and condemnation against us, unless it be prevented by the Divine mercy continually absolving us by a perpetual remission of our sins. Wherefore it will ever be true, as we asserted at the beginning, that if we be judged according to our demerits, whatever be our designs or undertakings, we are nevertheless with all our endeavors and all our pursuits, deserving of death and destruction.

XI. By Faith and Imputation—Opposed to the Papists' View

We must strenuously insist on these two points—first, that there never was an action performed by a pious man, which, if examined by the scrutinizing eye of Divine justice, would not deserve condemnation. And secondly, if any such thing be admitted (though it cannot be the case with any individual of mankind), yet being corrupted and contaminated by the sins, of which its performer is confessedly guilty, it loses every claim to the Divine favor. And this is the principal hinge on which our controversy (with the Papists) turns.

For concerning the beginning of justification, there is no dispute between us and the sounder schoolmen, but we all agree that a sinner being freely delivered from condemnation obtains righteousness, and that by the remission of his sins; only they, under the term *justification,* comprehend that renovation in which we are renewed by the Spirit of God to an obedience to the law, and so they describe the righteousness of a regenerate man as consisting in this—that a man, after having been once reconciled to God through faith in Christ, is accounted righteous with God on account of his good works, the merit of which is the cause of his acceptance. But the Lord, on the contrary, declares, "that faith was reckoned to Abraham for righteousness" (Rom. 4:9), not during the time while he yet remained a worshipper of idols, but after he had been eminent during many years for the sanctity of his life. Abraham, then, had for a long time worshipped God from a pure heart, and performed all that obedience to the law, which a mortal man is capable of performing; yet, after all, his righteousness consisted in faith. Whence we conclude, according to the argument of Paul, that it was not of works.

So when the prophet says, "The just shall live by his faith" (Hab. 2:4), he is not speaking of the impious and profane whom the Lord justifies by converting them to the faith; but his address is directed to believers, and they are promised life by faith. Paul also removes every doubt, when, in confirmation of this sentiment, he adduces the following passage of David: "Blessed are they whose iniquities are forgiven" (Rom. 4:7). But it is certain that David spoke not of impious men but of believers, whose characters resembled his own; for he spoke from the experience of his own conscience. Wherefore it is necessary for us, not to have this blessing for once only, but to retain it as long as we live.

Lastly, he asserts that the message of a free reconciliation with God is not only promulgated for a day or two, but is perpetual in the church (2 Cor. 5:18, 19). Believers, therefore, even to the end of their lives, have no other righteousness than that which is there described. For the mediatorial office is perpetually sustained by Christ, by whom the Father is reconciled to us; and the efficacy of whose death is perpetually the same, consisting in ablution, satisfaction, expiation, and perfect obedience, which covers all our iniquities. And Paul does not tell the Ephesians that they are indebted to grace merely for the beginning of their salvation, but that they "are saved by grace, not of works, lest any man should boast" (Eph. 2:8-9).

XII. Some Errors of the Schoolmen

The subterfuges by which the schoolmen endeavor to evade these arguments are unavailing. They say that the sufficiency of good works to justification arises not from their intrinsic merit, but from the grace through which they are accepted. Secondly, because they are constrained to acknowledge the righteousness of works to be always imperfect in the present state, they admit that as long as we live we need the remission of our sins, in order to supply the defects of our works; but that our deficiencies are compensated by works of supererogation. I reply that what they denominate the grace through which our works are accepted is no other than the free goodness of the Father with which he embraces us in Christ when he invests us with the righteousness of Christ, and accepts it as ours, in order that, in consequence of it, he may treat us as holy, pure, and righteous persons. For the righteousness of Christ (which, being the only perfect righteousness, is the only one that can bear the

Divine scrutiny) must be produced on our behalf, and judicially presented, as in the case of a surety. Being furnished with this, we obtain by faith the perpetual remission of our sins. Our imperfections and impurities, being concealed by its purity, are not imputed to us, but are as it were buried, and prevented from appearing in the view of Divine justice till the advent of that hour when the old man being slain and utterly annihilated in us, the Divine goodness shall receive us into a blessed peace with the new Adam, in that state to wait for the day of the Lord, when we shall receive incorruptible bodies, and be translated to the glories of the celestial kingdom.

XIII. The Impossibility of a "Partial" Righteousness

If these things are true, surely no works of ours can render us acceptable to God; nor can the actions themselves be pleasing to him, any otherwise than as a man, who is covered with the righteousness of Christ, pleases God and obtains the remission of his sins. For God has not promised eternal life as a reward of certain work; he only declares, that "he that does these things shall live" (Lev. 18:5; cf. Rom. 10:5), denouncing, on the contrary, that memorable curse against all who continue not in the observance of every one of his commands (Deut. 27:26; cf. Gal. 3:10). This abundantly refutes the erroneous notion of a partial righteousness, since no other righteousness is admitted into heaven but an entire observance of the law. Nor is there any more solidity in their pretense of a sufficient compensation for imperfections by works of supererogation. For are they not by this perpetually recurring to the subterfuge, from which they have already been driven, that the partial observance of the law constitutes, as far as it goes, a righteousness of works? They unblushingly assume as granted, what no man of sound judgment will concede.

The Lord frequently declares that he acknowledges no righteousness of works, except in a perfect obedience to his law. What presumption is it for us who are destitute of this, in order that we may not appear to be despoiled of all our glory, or, in other words, to submit entirely to the Lord—what presumption is it for us to boast of I know not what fragments of a few actions, and to endeavor to supply deficiencies by other satisfactions! Satisfactions have already been so completely demolished, that they ought not to occupy even a transient thought. I only remark that those who trifle in this manner do not consider what an execrable thing sin is in the sight of God; for indeed they ought to know that all the righteousness of all mankind, accumulated in one mass, is insufficient to compensate for a single sin. We see that man on account of one offense was rejected and abandoned by God, so that he lost all means of regaining salvation (Gen. 3). They are deprived, therefore, of the power of satisfaction, with which, however they flatter themselves, they will certainly never be able to render a satisfaction to God, to whom nothing will be pleasing or acceptable that proceeds from his enemies. Now, his enemies are all those to whom he determines to impute sin. Our sins, therefore, must be covered and forgiven before the Lord can regard any of our works. Whence it follows that the remission of sins is absolutely gratuitous, and that it is wickedly blasphemed by those who obtrude any satisfactions. Let us, therefore, after the example of the apostle, "for getting those things which are behind, and reaching forth unto those things which are before, press toward the mark for the prize of our high calling" (Phil. 3:13–14).

XIV. We Are but Servants of the Lord

But how is the pretense of works of supererogation consistent with this injunction—"When you shall have done all those things which are commanded you, say, 'We are unprofitable servants; we have done that which was our duty to do'" (Luke 17:10)? This direction does not inculcate an act of simulation or falsehood, but a decision in our mind respecting that of which we are certain. The Lord, therefore, commands us sincerely to think and consider with ourselves, that our services to him are none of them gratuitous, but merely the performance of indispensable duties; and that justly; for we are servants under such numerous obligations as we could never discharge; even though all our thoughts and all our members were devoted to the duties of the law. In saying, therefore, "When you shall have done all those things which are commanded," he supposes a case of one man having attained to a degree of righteousness beyond what is attained by all the men in the world.

How, then, while every one of us is at the greatest distance from this point, can we presume to glory that we have completely attained to that perfect standard? Nor can anyone reasonably object that there is nothing to prevent his efforts from going beyond his necessary obligations who, in any respect, fails of doing the duty incumbent on him. For we must acknowledge that we cannot imagine anything pertaining either to the service of God or to the love of our neighbor, which is not comprehended in the Divine law. But if it is a part of the law, let us not boast of voluntary liberality, where we are bound by necessity.

XV. Can There Be Any Boasting?

It is irrelevant to this subject, to allege the boasting of Paul (1 Cor. 9), that among the Corinthians he voluntarily receded from what, if he had chosen, he might have claimed as his right, and not only did what was incumbent on him to do, but afforded them his gratuitous services beyond the requisitions of duty. They ought to attend to the reason there assigned that he acted thus, "lest he should hinder the gospel of Christ" (1 Cor. 9:12). For wicked and fraudulent teachers recommended themselves by this stratagem of liberality by which they endeavored both to conciliate a favorable reception to their own pernicious dogmas, and to fix an odium on the gospel; so that Paul was necessitated either to endanger the doctrine of Christ, or to oppose these artifices.

Now, if it be a matter of indifference to a Christian to incur an offense when he may avoid it, I confess that the apostle performed for the Lord a work of supererogation; but if this was justly required of a prudent minister of the gospel, I maintain that he did what was his duty to do. Even if no such reason appeared, yet the observation of Chrysostom is always true—that all that we have is on the same tenure as the possessions of slaves, which the law pronounces to be the property of their masters. And Christ has clearly delivered the same truth in the parable, where he inquires whether we thank a servant, when he returns home in the evening, after the various labors of the day (Isa. 4:2). But it is possible that he may have labored with greater diligence than we had ventured to require. This may be granted; yet he has done no more than, by the condition of servitude, he was under an obligation to do; since he belongs to us, with all the ability he has. I say nothing of the nature of the supererogations which these men wish to boast of before God;

for they are contemptible trifles, which he has never commanded, which he does not approve, nor, when they render up their account to him, will he accept them. We cannot admit that there are any works of supererogation except such as those of which it is said by the prophet, "Who has required this at your hand" (Isa. 1:12)?

But let them remember the language of another passage respecting these things: "Wherefore do you spend money for that which is not bread? and your labor for that which satisfies not" (Isa. 4:2)? It is easy, indeed, for these idle doctors to dispute concerning these things in easy chairs; but when the Judge of all shall ascend the judgment seat, all such empty notions must vanish away. The object of our inquiries ought to be, what plea we may bring forward with confidence at his tribunal, not what we can invent in schools and cloisters.

XVI. No Confidence or Grounds for Boasting

On this subject our minds require to be guarded chiefly against two pernicious principles—That we place no confidence in the righteousness of our works, and that we ascribe no glory to them. The Scriptures everywhere drive us from all confidence when they declare that all our righteousnesses are odious in the Divine view, unless they are perfumed with the holiness of Christ; and that they can only excite the vengeance of God, unless they are supported by his merciful pardon. Thus they leave us nothing to do, but to deprecate the wrath of our Judge with the confession of David, "Enter not into judgment with your servant; for in your sight shall no man living be justified" (Psa. 143:2). And where Job says, "If I be wicked, woe unto me; and if I be righteous, yet will I not lift up my head" (Job 10:15); though he refers to that consummate righteousness of God, compared to

Justification by Faith

which even the angels are deficient, yet he at the same time shows that when God comes to judgment, all men must be dumb. For he not only means that he would rather freely recede than incur the danger of contending with the rigor of God, but signifies that he experiences in himself no other righteousness than what would instantaneously vanish before the Divine presence. When confidence is destroyed, all boasting must of necessity be relinquished. For who can give the praise of righteousness to his works, in which he is afraid to confide in the presence of God? We must therefore have recourse to the Lord in whom we are assured by Isaiah that, "all the seed of Israel shall be justified, and shall glory" (Isa. 45:25). For it is strictly true, as he says in another place, that we are "the planting of the Lord, that he might be glorified" (Isa. 41:3). Our minds therefore will then be properly purified when they shall in no degree confide nor glory in our works. But foolish men are led into such a false and delusive confidence by the error of always considering their works as the cause of their salvation.

XVII. We Have No Part in Causing Our Salvation

But if we advert to the four kinds of causes, which the philosophers direct us to consider in the production of effects, we shall find none of them consistent with works in the accomplishment of our salvation. For the Scripture everywhere proclaims that the efficient cause of eternal life being procured for us was the mercy of our heavenly Father, and his gratuitous love towards us; that the material cause is Christ and his obedience, by which he obtained a righteousness for us. And what shall we denominate the formal and instrumental cause, unless it be faith? These three John comprehends in one sentence, when he says that "God so loved the world that he gave his only begotten Son, that whosoever believes in him should not perish, but have everlasting life" (John 3:16).

The final cause the apostle declares to be, both the demonstration of the Divine righteousness and the praise of the Divine goodness, in a passage in which he also expressly mentions the other three causes. For this is his language to the Romans: "All have sinned, and come short of the glory of God, being justified freely by his grace" (Rom. 3:23ff.). Here we have the original source of our salvation, which is the gratuitous mercy of God towards us. It follows, "through the redemption that is in Christ Jesus"—here we have the matter of our justification. "Through faith in his blood"—here he points out the instrumental cause, by which the righteousness of Christ is revealed to us. Lastly, he subjoins the end of all when he says, "To declare his righteousness; that he might be just, and the justifier of him which believes in Jesus." And to suggest, by the way, that this righteousness consists in reconciliation or propitiation, he expressly asserts that Christ was "set forth to be a propitiation."

So also in the first chapter to the Ephesians, he teaches that we are received into the favor of God through his mere mercy; that it is accomplished by the mediation of Christ; that it is apprehended by faith; and that the end of all is, that the glory of the Divine goodness may be fully displayed (Eph. 1:5–7, 13). When we see that every part of our salvation is accomplished without us, what reason have we to confide or to glory in our works? Nor can even the most inveterate enemies of Divine grace raise any controversy with us concerning the efficient or the final cause, unless they mean altogether to renounce the authority of the Scripture. Over the material and formal causes they superinduce a false coloring; as if our own works were to share the honor of them with faith and the righteousness of Christ. But this also is contradicted by the Scripture, which affirms that Christ is the sole author of our righteousness and life, and that this blessing of righteousness is enjoyed by faith alone.

XVIII. On Affirming the Acceptance of the Saints

The saints often confirm and console themselves with the remembrance of their own innocence and integrity, and sometimes even refrain not from proclaiming it. Now, this is done for two reasons: either that, in comparing their good cause with the bad cause of the impious they derive from such comparison an assurance of victory, not so much by the commendation of their own righteousness, as by the just and merited condemnation of their adversaries; or that, even without any comparison with others, while they examine themselves before God, the purity of their consciences affords them some consolation and confidence. To the former of these reasons we shall advert hereafter; let us now briefly examine the consistency of the latter with what we have before asserted, that in the sight of God we ought to place no reliance on the merit of works, nor glory on account of them.

The consistency appears in this—that for the foundation and accomplishment of their salvation, the saints look to the Divine goodness alone without any regard to works. And they not only apply themselves to it above all things, as the commencement of their happiness, but likewise depend upon it as the consummation of their felicity. A conscience thus founded, built up, and established, is also confirmed by the consideration of works; that is, as far as they are evidences of God dwelling and reigning in us. Now, this confidence of works being found in none but those who have previously cast all the confidence of their souls on the mercy of God, it ought not to be thought contrary to that upon which it depends. Wherefore, when we exclude the confidence of works, we only mean that the mind of a Christian should not be directed to any merit of works as a mean of salvation; but should altogether rely on the gratuitous promise of righteousness. We do not forbid him to support and confirm this faith by marks of the Divine benevolence to him. For if, when we call to remembrance the various gifts which God has conferred on us, they are all as so many rays from the Divine countenance, by which we are illuminated to contemplate the full blaze of supreme goodness,—much more the grace of good works, which demonstrates that we have received the Spirit of adoption.

XIX. On Affirming the Adoption of the Saints

When the saints, therefore, confirm their faith, or derive matter of rejoicing from the integrity of their consciences, they only conclude from the fruits of vocation that they have been adopted by the Lord as his children. The declaration of Solomon that, "In the fear of the Lord is strong confidence" (Prov. 14:26); and the protestation sometimes used by the saints to obtain a favorable audience from the Lord that, "they have walked before" him "in truth and with a perfect heart" (2 Kings 20:3); these things have no concern in laying the foundation for establishing the conscience, nor are they of any value, except as they are consequences of the Divine vocation. For there nowhere exists that fear of God which can establish a full assurance, and the saints are conscious that their integrity is yet accompanied with many relics of corruption.

But as the fruits of regeneration evince that the Holy Spirit dwells in them, this affords them ample encouragement to expect the assistance of God in all their necessities, because they experience him to be their Father in an affair of such vast importance. And even this they cannot attain, unless they have first apprehended the Divine goodness, confirmed by no other assurance but that of the promise. For if they begin to estimate it by their good works, nothing will be weaker or more uncertain. For if their works be estimated in themselves, their imperfection will menace them with the wrath of God, as much as their purity, however incomplete, testifies his benevolence. In a word, they declare the benefits of God, but in such a way as not to turn away from his gratuitous favor, in which Paul assures us there is "length, and breadth, and depth, and height;" as though he had said, Which way so ever the pious turn their views, how high so ever they ascend, how widely so ever they expatiate, yet they ought not to go beyond the love of Christ, but employ themselves wholly in meditating on it, because it comprehends in itself all dimensions. Therefore he says that it "passes knowledge," and that when we know how much Christ has loved us, we are "filled with all the fullness of God" (Eph. 3:18-19). So also in another place, when he glories that believers are victorious in every conflict, he immediately adds, as the reason of it, "through him that loved us" (Rom. 8:37).

XX. The Saints' Confidence in the Works of God Alone

We see now that the confidence which the saints have in their works is not such as either ascribes anything to the merit of them (since they view them only as the gifts of God, in which they acknowledge his goodness, and as marks of their, calling, whence they infer their election), or derogates the least from the gratuitous righteousness which we obtain in Christ; since it depends upon it, and cannot subsist without it. This is concisely and beautifully represented by Augustine, when he says,

> I do not say to the Lord, Despise not the works of my hands. I have sought the Lord with my hands, and I have not been deceived. But I commend not the works of my hands; for I fear that when you have examined them, you will find more sin than merit. This only I say, this I ask, this I desire; Despise not the works of your hands. Behold in me your work, not mine. For if you behold mine, you condemn me; if you behold your own, you crown me. Because whatever good works I have, they are from you.[3]

He assigns two reasons why he ventured not to boast of his works to God. First, that if he has any good ones, he sees nothing of his own in them. Secondly, that even these are buried under a multitude of sins. Hence the conscience experiences more fear and consternation than security. Therefore he desires God to behold his best performances, only that he may recognize in them the grace of his own calling, and perfect the work which he has begun.

XXI. God's Goodness: The Only Cause for Justification

The remaining objection is that the Scripture represents the good works of believers as the causes for which the Lord blesses them. But this must be understood so as not to affect what we have before proved, that the efficient cause of our salvation is the love of God the Father; the material cause, the obedience of the Son; the instrumental cause, the illumination of the Spirit,

---

[3] Augustine, *Expositions on the Psalms*, 137.

that is, faith; and the final cause, the glory of the infinite goodness of God. No obstacle arises from these things to prevent good works being considered by the Lord as inferior causes. But how does this happen?

Because those whom his mercy has destined to the inheritance of eternal life, he, in his ordinary dispensations, introduces to the possession of it by good works. That which, in the order of his dispensations, precedes, he denominates the cause of that which follows. For this reason he sometimes deduces eternal life from works; not that the acceptance of it is to be referred to them; but because he justifies the objects of his election, that he may finally glorify them; he makes the former favor, which is a step to the succeeding one, in some sense the cause of it. But whenever the true cause is to be assigned, he does not direct us to take refuge in works, but confines our thoughts entirely to his mercy. For what does he teach us by the apostle? "The wages of sin is death; but the gift of God is eternal life through Jesus Christ our Lord" (Rom. 6:23). Why does he not oppose righteousness to sin, as well as life to death? Why does he not make righteousness the cause of life, as well as sin the cause of death? For then the antithesis would have been complete, whereas by this variation it is partly destroyed. But the apostle intended by this comparison to express a certain truth—that death is due to the demerits of men, and that life proceeds solely from the mercy of God.

Lastly, these phrases denote rather the order of the Divine gifts, than the cause of them. In the accumulation of graces upon graces, God derives from the former a reason for adding the next, that he may not omit anything necessary to the enrichment of his servants. And while he thus pursues his liberality, he would have us always to remember his gratuitous election, which is the source and original of all. For although he loves the gifts which he daily confers, as emanations from that fountain, yet it is our duty to adhere to that gratuitous acceptance, which alone can support our souls, and to connect the gifts of his Spirit, which he afterwards bestows on us, with the first cause, in such a manner as will not be derogatory to it.

5

Boasting of the Merit of Works, Equally Subversive of God's Glory in the Gift of Righteousness, and of the Certainty of Salvation

We have now discussed the principal branch of this subject; that because righteousness, if dependent on works, must inevitably be confounded in the sight of God, therefore it is contained exclusively in the mercy of God and the participation of Christ, and consequently in faith alone.

I. Do Works Merit Favor with God?
Now, it must be carefully remarked that this is the principal hinge on which the argument turns, that we may not be implicated in the common delusion, which equally affects the learned and the vulgar. For as soon as justification by faith or works becomes the subject of inquiry, they have immediate recourse to those passages which seem to attribute to works some degree of merit in the sight of God; as though justification by works would be fully evinced, if they could be proved to be of any value before God. We have already clearly demonstrated that the righteousness of works consists only in a perfect and complete observance of the law. Whence it follows that no man is justified by works, but he who, being elevated to the summit

of perfection, cannot be convicted even of the least transgression. This, therefore, is a different and separate question, whether, although works be utterly insufficient for the justification of men, they do not, nevertheless, merit the grace of God.

II. On the Term "Merit"

In the first place, with respect to the term *merit*, it is necessary for me to premise that whoever first applied it to human works, as compared with the Divine judgment, showed very little concern for the purity of the faith. I gladly abstain from all controversies about mere words; but I could wish that this sobriety had always been observed by Christian writers, that they had avoided the unnecessary adoption of terms not used in the Scriptures, and calculated to produce great offense, but very little advantage.

For what necessity was there for the introduction of the word *merit*, when the value of good works might be significantly expressed without offense by a different term? But the great offense contained in it, appears in the great injury the world has received from it. The consummate haughtiness of its import can only obscure the Divine grace, and taint the minds of men with presumptuous arrogance. I confess, the ancient writers of the Church have generally used it, and I wish that their misuse of one word had not been the occasion of error to posterity. Yet they also declare in some places that they did not intend anything prejudicial to the truth. For this is the language of Augustine in one passage: "Let human merit, which was lost by Adam, here be silent, and let the grace of God reign through

Jesus Christ."[1] Again: "The saints ascribe nothing to their own merits; they will ascribe all, O God, only to your mercy."[2] In another place: "And when a man sees that whatever good he has, he has it not from himself, but from his God, he sees that all that is commended in him proceeds not from his own merits, but from the Divine mercy."[3] We see how, by divesting man of the power of performing good actions, he likewise destroys the dignity of merit. Chrysostom says, "Our works, if there be any consequent on God's gratuitous vocation, are a retribution and a debt; but the gifts of God are grace, beneficence, and immense liberality."

Leaving the name, however, let us rather attend to the thing. I have before cited a passage from Bernard: "As not to presume on our merits is sufficiently meritorious, so to be destitute of merits is sufficient for the judgment." But by the explanation immediately annexed, he properly softens the harshness of these expressions, when he says,

> Therefore you should be concerned to have merits; and if you have them, you should know that they are given to you; you should hope for the fruit, the mercy of God; and you have escaped all danger of poverty, ingratitude, and presumption. Happy the Church which is not destitute, either of merits without presumption, or of presumption without merits.

And just before he had fully shown how pious his meaning was. "For concerning merits," he says, "why should the Church be solicitous, which has a more firm and secure

---

[1] Augustine, *The Predestination of the Saints*
[2] Augustine, *Expositions on the Psalms*, 139.
[3] Ibid., 88.

foundation for glorying in the purpose of God? For God cannot deny himself; he will perform what he has promised. Thus you have no reason for inquiring, on account of what merits we may hope for blessings, especially when you read, 'Not for your sakes, but for my sake' [Ezek. 36:32]; it is sufficiently meritorious to know that merits are insufficient."[4]

III. Why Good Works Please God

The Scripture shows what all our works are capable of meriting, when it represents them as unable to bear the Divine scrutiny, because they are full of impurity; and in the next place, what would be merited by the perfect observance of the law, if this could anywhere be found, when it directs us, "When you shall have done all those things which are commanded you, say, 'We are unprofitable servants'" (Luke 17:10); because we shall not have conferred any favor on God, but only have performed the duties incumbent on us, for which no thanks are due.

Nevertheless, the good works which the Lord has conferred on us, he denominates our own, and declares that he will not only accept, but also reward them. It is our duty to be animated by so great a promise, and to stir up our minds that we "be not weary in well doing" (Gal. 6:9; 2 Thes. 3:13), and to be truly grateful for so great an instance of Divine goodness. It is beyond a doubt that whatever is laudable in our works proceeds from the grace of God; and that we cannot properly ascribe the least portion of it to ourselves. If we truly and seriously acknowledge this truth, not only all confidence, but likewise all idea of merit, immediately vanishes.

---

[4] Bernard, *Sermons on the Song of Songs*, serm. 98.

We, I say, do not, like the sophists, divide the praise of good works between God and man, but we preserve it to the Lord complete, entire, and uncontaminated. All that we attribute to man is that those works which were otherwise good are tainted and polluted by his impurity. For nothing proceeds from the most perfect man, which is wholly immaculate. Therefore let the Lord sit in judgment on the best of human actions, and he will indeed recognize in them his own righteousness, but man's disgrace and shame. Good works, therefore, are pleasing to God, and not unprofitable to the authors of them; and they will moreover receive the most ample blessings from God as their reward; not because they merit them, but because the Divine goodness has freely appointed them this reward.

But what wickedness is it, not to be content with that Divine liberality which remunerates works destitute of merit with unmerited rewards, but with sacrilegious ambition still to aim at more, that what entirely originates in the Divine munificence may appear to be a compensation of the merit of works! Here I appeal to the common sense of every man. If he who, by the liberality of another, enjoys the use and profit of an estate, usurp to himself also the title of proprietor, does he not by such ingratitude deserve to lose the possession which he had?

So also if a slave, manumitted by his master, conceal his mean condition as a freed-man, and boast that he was free by birth, does he not deserve to be reduced to his former servitude? For this is the legitimate way of enjoying a benefit, if we neither arrogate more than is given us, nor defraud our benefactor of his due praise; but, on the contrary, conduct ourselves in such a manner, that what he has conferred on us may appear, as it were, to continue with himself. If this moderation ought to be observed towards men, let everyone examine and consider what is due to God.

IV. Answering Objections from the Sophists

I know that the sophists abuse some texts in order to prove that the term *merit* is found in the Scriptures with reference to God. They cite a passage from Ecclesiasticus: "Mercy shall make place for every man according to the merit of his works" (Ecclus. 16:14). And from the Epistle to the Hebrews: "To do good, and to communicate, forget not; for with such sacrifices men merit of God" (Heb. 13:16).

My right to reject the authority of Ecclesiasticus, I at present relinquish; but I deny that they faithfully cite the words of the writer of Ecclesiasticus, whoever he might be. For in the Greek copy it is as follows: *Pasē eleēmosynē poiēsei topon; hekastos gar kata ta erga hautou heurēsei* (He shall make place for every mercy; and every man shall find according to his works). And that this is the genuine reading, which is corrupted in the Latin version, appears both from the complexion of the words themselves and from the preceding context. In the passage quoted from the Epistle to the Hebrews, there is no reason why they should endeavor to ensnare us by a single word, when the apostle's words in the Greek imply nothing more than that "with such sacrifices God is well pleased." This alone ought to be abundantly sufficient to repress and subdue the insolence of our pride, that we transgress not the scriptural rule by ascribing any dignity to human works.

Moreover, the doctrine of the Scripture is that our good works are perpetually defiled with many blemishes, which might justly offend God and incense him against us; so far are they from being able to conciliate his favor, or to excite his beneficence towards us; yet that, because in his great mercy he does not examine them according to the rigor of his justice, he accepts them as though they were immaculately pure, and therefore rewards them, though void of all merit, with infinite blessings both in this life and in that which is to come. For I cannot admit the distinction laid down by some who are otherwise men of learning and piety, that good works merit the graces which are conferred on us in this life, and that eternal salvation is the reward of faith alone; because the Lord almost always places the reward of labors and the crown of victory in heaven.

Besides, to ascribe the accumulation of graces upon graces, given us by the Lord, to the merit of works, in such a manner as to detract it from grace, is contrary to the doctrine of the Scripture. For though Christ says, that "to everyone that has shall be given," and that "the good and faithful servant, who has been faithful over a few things, shall be made ruler over many things" (Matt. 25:21, 29), yet he likewise shows in another place that the improvements of believers are the gifts of his gratuitous kindness. "Ho, every one that thirsts," says he, "come you to the waters, and he that has no money; come you, buy, and eat; yea, come, buy wine and milk without money and without price" (Isa. 55:1). Whatever, therefore, is now conferred on believers to promote their salvation as well as their future blessedness, flows exclusively from the beneficence of God; nevertheless he declares that both in the latter and in the former, he has respect to our works, because, to demonstrate the magnitude of his love to us, he dignifies with such honor, not only ourselves, but even the gifts which he has bestowed on us.

V. Christ is Our Righteousness

If these points had been handled and digested in proper order in former ages, there would never have arisen so many debates and dissensions. Paul says that, in erecting the super structure of Christian doctrine, it is necessary to retain that foundation which he had laid among the Corinthians, other than which no man can lay, which is Jesus Christ (1 Cor. 3:10, 11). What kind of a foundation have we in Christ? Has he begun our salvation, that we may complete it ourselves? and has he merely opened a way for us to proceed in by our own powers? By no means!

But, as the apostle before stated, when we acknowledge him, he is "made unto us righteousness" (1 Cor. 1:30). No man, therefore, is properly founded on Christ, but he who has complete righteousness in him; since the apostle says that he was sent, not to assist us in the attainment of righteousness, but to be himself our righteousness; that is to say, that we were chosen in him from eternity, before the formation of the world, not on account of any merit of ours, but according to the purpose of the Divine will (Eph. 1:3-5); that by the death of Christ we are redeemed from the sentence of death, and liberated from perdition (Col. 1:14, 20, 21); that in him we are adopted as sons and heirs by the heavenly Father (John 1:12), to whom we have been reconciled by his blood; that being committed to his protection, we are not in the least danger of perishing (John 10:28, 29); that being thus grafted into him, we are already, as it were, partakers of eternal life, and entered by hope into the kingdom of God; and moreover, that having obtained such a participation of him, however foolish we may be in ourselves, he is our wisdom before God; that however impure we are, he is our purity; that though we are weak and exposed to Satan, yet that power is ours which is given to him in heaven and in earth (Matt. 28:18), by which he defeats Satan for us, and breaks the gates of hell; that though we still carry about with us a body of death, yet he is our life.

In short, that all that is his belongs to us, and that we have everything in him, but nothing in ourselves. On this foundation, I say, it is necessary for us to build, if we wish to "grow unto a holy temple in the Lord" (Eph. 2:21; cf. Titus 3:7).

VI. The Sophist Error that Diminishes the Merit of Christ

But the world has long been taught a different lesson. For I know not what good works of morality have been invented to render men acceptable to God before they are grafted into Christ. As though the Scripture were false in asserting that "he that has not the Son of God, has not life" (1 John 5:12). If they are destitute of life, how could they generate any cause of life? As though there were no truth in the declaration that "whatsoever is not of faith is sin!" (Rom. 14:23); as though an evil tree could produce good fruits!

But what room have these most pestilent sophists left to Christ for the exertion of his power? They say that he has merited for us the first grace; that is, the opportunity of meriting; and that now it is our part not to miss the offered opportunity. What extreme impudence and impiety! Who would have expected that any persons professing the name of Christ would presume thus to rob him of his power, and almost to trample him under their feet? It is everywhere testified of him, that all who believe in him are justified (Acts 13:39). These men tell us that the only benefit received from him is that a way is opened for all men to justify themselves. But I wish that they had experienced what is contained in these passages: "He that has the Son, has life" (1 John 5:12); "he that believes is passed from death unto life" (John 5:24); "justified by his grace," that we might "be made heirs of eternal life" (Rom. 3:24); that believers have Christ abiding in them, by whom they are united to God (1 John 3:24); that they are partakers of his life, and sit with him "in heavenly places" (Eph. 2:6); that they are translated into the kingdom of God, and have obtained salvation (Col. 1:13); and innumerable places of similar import.

For they do not signify that by faith in Christ we merely gain the ability to attain righteousness or effect our salvation, but that both are bestowed on us. Therefore, as soon as we are grafted into Christ by faith, we are already become sons of God, heirs of heaven, partakers of righteousness, possessors of life, and (the better to refute their falsehoods) we have attained, not the opportunity of meriting, but all the merits of Christ; for they are all communicated to us.

VII. Further Refutations to the Sophists

Thus the Sorbonic[5] schools, those sources of all kinds of errors, have deprived us of justification by faith, which is the substance of all piety. They grant, indeed, in words, that a man is justified by faith formed; but this they afterwards explain to be, because faith renders good works effectual to justification; so that their mention of faith has almost the appearance of mockery, since it could not be passed over in silence, while the Scripture is so full of it, without exposing them to great censure.

And not content with this, they rob God of part of the praise of good works, and transfer it to man. Perceiving that good works avail but little to the exaltation of man, and that they cannot properly be denominated merits if they be considered as

---

[5] Collège de Sorbonne (est. 1257) in Paris, France; a 16th century stronghold of Catholic ideology.

the effects of Divine grace, they derive them from the power of free will; which is like extracting oil from a stone. They contend that though grace be the principal cause of them, yet that this is not to the exclusion of free-will, from which all merit originates. And this is maintained not only by the latter sophists, but likewise by their master, Lombard, whom, when compared with them, we may pronounce to be sound and sober.

Truly wonderful was their blindness, with Augustine so frequently in their mouths, not to see how solicitously he endeavored to prevent men from arrogating the least degree of glory on account of good works. Before, when we discussed the question of free-will, we cited from him some testimonies to this purpose; and similar ones frequently recur in his writings; as when he forbids us ever to boast of our merits, since even they are the gifts of God; and when he says, "that all our merit proceeds from grace alone; that it is not obtained by our sufficiency, but is produced entirely by grace,"[6] &c. That Lombard was blind to the light of Scripture, in which he appears not to have been so well versed, need not excite so much surprise.

Yet nothing could be wished for more explicit, in opposition to him and his disciples, than this passage of the apostle; who, having interdicted Christians from all boasting, subjoins as a reason why boasting is unlawful, that "we are his (God's) workmanship, created in Christ Jesus unto good works, which God has before ordained that we should walk in them" (Eph. 2:10). Since nothing good, then, can proceed from us but as we are regenerated, and our regeneration is, without exception,

---

[6] Augustine, *Expositions on the Psalms*, 104; *Letters*, 105.

entirely of God, we have no right to arrogate to ourselves the smallest particle of our good works.

Lastly, while they assiduously inculcate good works, they at the same time instruct the consciences of men in such a manner, that they can never dare to be confident that God is propitious and favorable to their works. But, on the contrary, our doctrine, without any mention of merit, animates the minds of believers with peculiar consolation, while we teach them that their works are pleasing to God, and that their persons are undoubtedly accepted by him. And we likewise require that no man attempt or undertake any work without faith; that is, unless he can previously determine, with a certain confidence of mind, that it will be pleasing to God.

VIII. Restatement of the Foundation of Justification

Wherefore let us not suffer ourselves to be seduced even a hair's breadth from the only foundation on which, when it is laid, wise architects erect a firm and regular superstructure. For if there be a necessity for doctrine and exhortation, they apprize us that "for this purpose the Son of God was manifested, that he might destroy the works of the devil; whosoever is born of God does not commit sin" (1 John 3:8, 9); "the time past of our life may suffice us to have wrought the will of the Gentiles" (1 Pet. 4:3); the elect of God are vessels of mercy selected to honor, and therefore ought to be cleansed from all impurity (2 Tim. 2:20; cf. Rom. 9:23).

But everything is said at once, when it is shown that Christ chooses such for his disciples as will deny themselves, take up their cross, and follow him (Luke 9:23). He who has denied himself has laid the axe to the root of all evils, that he may no longer seek those things which are his own; he who has taken up his cross, has prepared himself for all patience and gentleness. But the example of Christ comprehends not only these, but all other duties of piety and holiness. He was obedient to his Father, even to death; he was entirely occupied in performing the works of God; he aspired with his whole soul to promote the glory of his Father; he laid down his life for his brethren; he both acted and prayed for the benefit of his enemies.

But if there be need of consolation, these passages will afford it in a wonderful degree: "We are troubled on every side, yet not distressed; we are perplexed, but not in despair; persecuted, but not forsaken; cast down, but not destroyed; always bearing about in the body the dying of the Lord Jesus, that the life also of Jesus might be made manifest in our body" (2 Cor. 4:8-10). "If we be dead with him, we shall also live with him; if we suffer, we shall also reign with him" (2 Tim. 2:11, 12). "Being made conformable unto his death; if by any means I might attain unto the resurrection of the dead" (Phil. 3:10-11). The Father has predestinated all whom he has chosen in his Son "to be conformed to his image, that he might be the first-born among many brethren;" and therefore "neither death, nor life, nor things present, nor things to come, shall separate us from the love of God which is in Christ Jesus" (Rom. 8:29, 38, 39); but "all things shall work together for good" (Rom. 8:28) to us, and conduce to our salvation. We do not justify men by works before God; but we say, that all who are of God are regenerated and made new creatures, that they may depart from the kingdom of sin into the kingdom of righteousness; and that by this testimony they ascertain their vocation (2 Pet. 1:10), and, like trees, are judged by their fruits.

6

A Refutation of the Injurious Calumnies of the Papists Against This Doctrine

The observation with which we closed the preceding chapter is, of itself, sufficient to refute the impudence of some impious persons, who accuse us, in the first place, of destroying good works, and seducing men from the pursuit of them, when we say that they are not justified by works, nor saved through their own merit; and secondly, of making too easy a road to righteousness, when we teach that it consists in the gratuitous remission of sins; and of enticing men, by this allurement, to the practice of sin, to which they have naturally too strong a propensity. These calumnies, I say, are sufficiently refuted by that one observation; yet I will briefly reply to them both.

I. Calumnies of the Papists

They allege that *justification by faith* destroys good works. I forbear any remarks on the characters of these zealots for good works who thus calumniate us. Let them rail with impunity as licentiously as they infest the whole world with the impurity of their lives. They affect to lament that while faith is so magnificently extolled, works are degraded from their proper rank. What if they be more encouraged and established? For we never dream either of a faith destitute of good works, or of a justification unattended by them. This is the sole difference that, while we acknowledge a necessary connection between faith and good works, we attribute justification not to works, but to faith. Our reason for this we can readily explain, if we only turn to Christ, towards whom faith is directed, and from whom it receives all its virtue. Why, then, are we justified by faith? Because by faith we apprehend the righteousness of Christ, which is the only medium of our reconciliation to God.

But this you cannot attain without at the same time attaining to sanctification. For he "is made unto us wisdom and righteousness, and sanctification and redemption" (1 Cor. 1:30). Christ therefore justifies no one whom he does not also sanctify. For these benefits are perpetually and indissolubly connected, so that whom he illuminates with his wisdom, them he redeems; whom he redeems, he justifies; whom he justifies, he sanctifies. But as the present question relates only to righteousness and sanctification, let us insist upon them. We may distinguish between them, but Christ contains both inseparably in himself. Do you wish, then, to obtain righteousness in Christ? You must first possess Christ; but you cannot possess him without becoming a partaker of his sanctification; for he cannot be divided. Since, then, the Lord affords us the enjoyment of these blessings only in the bestowment of himself, he gives them both together, and never one without the other. Thus we see how true it is that we are justified, not without works, yet not by works; since union with Christ, by which we are justified, contains sanctification as well as righteousness.

II. Refuting the Discouraged of Good Works

It is also exceedingly false that the minds of men are seduced from an inclination to virtue by our divesting them of all ideas of merit. Here the reader must just be informed that they impertinently argue from reward to merit, as I shall afterwards more fully explain; because, in fact, they are ignorant of this principle that God is equally liberal in assigning a reward to good works, as in imparting an ability to perform them. But this I would rather defer to its proper place.

It will suffice, at present, to show the weakness of their objection, which shall be done two ways. For, first, when they say that there will be no concern about the proper regulation of our life without a hope of reward being proposed, they altogether deceive themselves. If they only mean that men serve God in expectation of a reward, and hire or sell their services to him, they gain but little; for he will be freely worshipped and freely loved, and he approves of that worshipper who, after being deprived of all hope of receiving any reward, still ceases not to worship him. Besides, if men require to be stimulated, it is impossible to urge more forcible arguments than those which arise from the end of our redemption and calling; such as the word of God adduces, when it inculcates, that it is the greatest and most impious ingratitude not reciprocally to "love him who first loved us" (1 John 4:10, 19); that "by the blood of Christ our consciences are purged from dead works, to serve the living God" (Heb. 9:14); that it is a horrible sacrilege, after having been once purged, to defile ourselves with new pollutions, and to profane that sacred blood (Heb. 10:29); that we have been "delivered out of the hand of our enemies," that we "might serve him without fear, in holiness and righteousness before him, all the days of our life" (Luke 1:74–75); that we are made "free from sin," that with a free spirit we might "become the servants of righteousness" (Rom. 6:18); "that our old man is crucified," that "we should walk in newness of life" (Rom. 6:4, 6). Again: "If you've been risen with Christ," as his members indeed are, "seek those things which are above," and conduct yourselves as "pilgrims on the earth;" that you may aspire towards heaven, where your treasure is (Col. 3:1; cf. Heb. 11:13; 1 Pet. 2:11). That "the grace of God has appeared, teaching us, that denying ungodliness and worldly lusts, we should live soberly, righteously, and godly, in this present world; looking for that blessed hope, and the glorious appearing of the great God and our Savior" (Titus 2:11-13). Wherefore, "God has not appointed us to wrath, but to obtain salvation by Christ" (1 Thes. 5:9). That we are the "temples of the Holy Ghost," which it is unlawful to profane (1 Cor. 3:16-17; 6:19; Eph. 2:21); that we are not *darkness*, "but light in the Lord," whom it becomes to "walk as children of the light" (Eph. 5:8); that "God has not called us unto uncleanness, but unto holiness; for this is the will of God, even our sanctification, that we should abstain from fornication (1 Thes. 4:3, 7); that our calling is a holy one, which should be followed by a correspondent purity of life (2 Tim. 1:9; 1 Pet. 1:15); that we are "made free from sin," that we might "become servants of righteousness" (Rom. 6:18).

Can we be incited to charity by any stronger argument than that of John, "If God so loved us, we ought also to love one another?" "in this the children of God are manifest, and the children of the devil" (1 John 4:11; 3:10); hereby the children of light, by their abiding in love, are distinguished from the children of darkness; or that of Paul, that if we be united to Christ, we are members of one body, and ought to afford each other mutual assistance (1 Cor. 12:12, &c.)? Or can we be more powerfully excited to holiness than when we are informed by John that "every man that has this hope in him purifies himself, even as God is pure" (1 John 3:3)? Or when Paul says, "Having therefore these promises (relative to our adoption), let us cleanse ourselves from all filthiness of the flesh and spirit" (2 Cor. 7:1)? or than when we hear Christ proposing himself as our example, that we should follow his steps (Matt. 11:29; John 13:15)?

III. Salvation Depends on God's Mercy

These few instances, indeed, I have given as a specimen. For if I were disposed to quote every particular passage, I should produce a large volume. The apostles are quite full of admonitions, exhortations, and reproofs, to "furnish the man of God unto all good works" (2 Tim. 3:17), and that without any mention of merit. But they rather deduce their principal exhortations from this consideration that our salvation depends not on any merit of ours, but merely on the mercy of God. As Paul, after having very largely shown that we can have no hope of life, but from the righteousness of Christ, when he proceeds to exhortations, beseeches us "by the mercies of God" with which we have been favored (Rom. 12:1). And indeed this one reason ought to be enough; that God may be glorified in us (Matt. 5:16).

But if any persons be not so powerfully affected by the glory of God, yet the remembrance of his benefits should be amply sufficient to incite them to rectitude of conduct. But these men, who by the obtrusion of merit extort some servile and constrained acts of obedience to the law, are guilty of falsehood when they affirm that we have no arguments to enforce the practice of good works, because we do not proceed in the same way; as though, truly, such obedience were very pleasing to God, who declares that he "loves a cheerful giver;" and forbids anything to be given "grudgingly, or of necessity" (2 Cor. 9:7). Nor do I say this because I either reject or neglect that kind of exhortation which the Scripture frequently uses, that no method of animating us to our duty may be omitted. It mentions the reward which "God will render to every man according to his works" (Matt. 16:27; Rom. 2:6), but that this is the only argument, or the principal one, I deny.

In the next place, I assert that we ought not to begin with it. Moreover, I contend that it has no tendency to establish the merit preached by these men, as we shall afterwards see; and, lastly, that it is entirely useless, unless preceded by this doctrine, that we are justified solely on account of the merit of Christ, apprehended by faith, and not on account of any merit in our own works; because none can be capable of the pursuit of holiness, but such as have previously imbibed this doctrine. This sentiment is beautifully suggested by the Psalmist when he thus addresses the Lord: "There is forgiveness with you, that you may be feared" (Psa. 130:4). For he shows that there is no worship of God without an acknowledgment of his mercy, on which alone it is both founded and established. And this well deserves to be remarked, in order that we may know, not only that the true worship of God arises from a reliance on his mercy, but that the fear of God (which the Papists hold to be meritorious) cannot be dignified with the title of *merit*, because it is founded in the pardon and remission of sins.

IV. God Alone Can Grant Remission of Sins

But the most futile of all their calumnies is that men are encouraged to the practice of sin by our maintaining the gratuitous remission of sins, in which we make righteousness to consist. For we say that so great a blessing could never be compensated by any virtue of ours, and that therefore it could never be obtained, unless it were gratuitously bestowed. Moreover, that it is gratuitous to us indeed, but not so to Christ, whom it cost so much, even his own most sacred blood, beside which no price sufficiently valuable could be paid to Divine justice. When men are taught in this manner, they are apprized that it is not owing to them that this most sacred blood is not shed as often as they sin. Besides, we learn that such is our pollution, that it can never be washed away, except in the fountain of this immaculate blood. Must not persons who hear these things conceive a greater horror of sin, than if it were said to be cleansed by a sprinkling of good works? And if they have any fear of God, will they not dread, after being once purified, to plunge themselves again into the mire, and thereby to disturb and infect, as far as they can, the purity of this fountain? "I have washed my feet," (says the believing soul in Solomon,) "how shall I defile them" (Songs 5:3)?

Now, it is plain which party better deserves the charge of degrading the value of remission of sins, and prostituting the dignity of righteousness. They pretend that God is appeased by their frivolous *satisfactions*, which are no better than dung. We assert that the guilt of sin is too atrocious to be expiated by such insignificant trifles; that the displeasure of God is too great to be appeased by these worthless satisfactions; and therefore that this is the exclusive prerogative of the blood of Christ. They say that righteousness, if it ever be defective, is restored and repaired by works of satisfaction. We think it so valuable that no compensation of works can be adequate to it; and therefore that for its restitution we must have recourse to the mercy of God alone. The remaining particulars that pertain to the remission of sins may be found in the next chapter.

7

THE HARMONY BETWEEN THE PROMISES OF THE LAW AND THOSE OF THE GOSPEL

I. Summary of Previous Arguments

Let us now pursue the other arguments with which Satan by his satellites attempts to destroy or to weaken justification by faith. I think we have already gained this point with these calumniators—that they can no longer accuse us of being enemies to good works. For we reject the notion of justification by works, not that no good works may be done, or that those which are performed may be denied to be good, but that we may neither confide in them, nor glory in them, nor ascribe salvation to them. For this is our trust, this is our glory, and the only anchor of our salvation, that Christ the Son of God is ours, and that we are likewise, in him, sons of God and heirs of the celestial kingdom; being called, not for our worthiness, but by the Divine goodness, to the hope of eternal felicity. But since they assail us besides, as we have observed, with other weapons, let us also proceed to the repulsion of them.

In the first place, they return to the legal promises which the Lord gave to the observers of his law, and inquire whether we suppose them to be entirely vain, or of any validity. As it would be harsh and ridiculous to say they are vain, they take it for granted that they have some efficacy. Hence they argue that we are not justified by faith alone. For thus says the Lord, "Wherefore it shall come to pass, if you hearken to these judgments, and keep and do them, that the Lord your God shall keep unto you the covenant and the mercy which he swore unto your fathers; and he will love you, and bless you, and multiply you" (Deut. 7:12-13). Again: "If you thoroughly amend your ways and your doings; if you thoroughly execute judgment between a man and his neighbor; if you oppress not, neither walk after other gods; then will I cause you to dwell in this place" &c. (Jer. 7:5-7). I am not willing to recite a thousand passages of the same kind, which, not being different in sense, will be elucidated by an explanation of these. The sum of all is declared by Moses, who says that in the law are proposed "a blessing and a curse, life and death" (Deut. 11:26; 30:15).

Now, they argue, either that this blessing becomes inefficacious and nugatory, or that justification is not by faith alone. We have already shown how, if we adhere to the law, being destitute of every blessing, we are obnoxious to the curse which is denounced on all transgressors. For the Lord promises nothing, except to the perfect observers of his law, of which description not one can be found. The consequence, then, is that all mankind are proved by the law to be obnoxious to the curse and wrath of God; in order to be saved from which, they need deliverance from the power of the law, and emancipation from its servitude; not a carnal liberty, which would seduce us from obedience to the law, invite to all kinds of licentiousness, break down the barriers of inordinate desire, and give the reins to every lawless passion; but a spiritual liberty, which will console and elevate a distressed and dejected conscience, showing it to be delivered from the curse and condemnation under which it was held by the law. This liberation from subjection to the law, and manumission (if I may use the term), we attain when we apprehend by faith the mercy of God in Christ, by which we are assured of the remission of sins, by the sense of which the law penetrated us with compunction and remorse.

II. Confirming Justification by Faith Apart from Works

For this reason all the promises of the law would be ineffectual and vain, unless we were assisted by the goodness of God in the gospel. For the condition of a perfect obedience to the law, on which they depend, and in consequence of which alone they are to be fulfilled, will never be performed. Now, the Lord affords this assistance, not by leaving a part of righteousness in our works, and supplying part from his mercy, but by appointing Christ alone for the completion of righteousness. For the apostle, having said that he and other Jews, "knowing that a man is not justified by the works of the law, believed in Christ," adds as a reason, not that they might be assisted to obtain a complete righteousness by faith in Christ, but "that they might be justified by the faith of Christ, and not by the works of the law" (Gal. 2:16). If the faithful pass from the law to faith, to find righteousness in the latter, which they perceive to be wanting in the former, they certainly renounce the righteousness of the law. Therefore let whosoever will now amplify the rewards which are said to await the observer of the law; only let him remark, that our depravity prevents us from receiving any benefit from them, till we have obtained by faith another righteousness.

Thus David, after having mentioned the reward which the Lord has prepared for his servants, immediately proceeds to the acknowledgment of sins, by which it is annulled. In the nineteenth psalm, likewise, he magnificently celebrates the benefits of the law; but immediately exclaims, "Who can understand his errors? cleanse thou me from secret faults" (Psa. 19:12). This passage perfectly accords with that before referred to, where, after having said, "All the paths of the Lord are mercy and truth unto such as keep his covenant and his testimonies," he adds, "For your name's sake, O Lord, pardon mine iniquity; for it is great" (Psa. 25:10-11). So we ought also to acknowledge that the Divine favor is offered to us in the law, if we could purchase it by our works; but that no merit of ours can ever obtain it.

III. The True Value of Works vs. the Sophists' View

What, then, it will be said, were those promises given to vanish away without producing any effect? I have already declared that this is not my opinion. I assert, indeed, that they have no efficacy with respect to us as long as they are referred to the merit of works; wherefore, considered in themselves, they are in some sense abolished. Thus that grand promise, "Keep my statutes and judgments; which if a man do, he shall live in them" (Lev. 18:5); the apostle maintains to be of no value to us, if we rest upon it, and that it will be no more beneficial to us than if it had never been given; because it is inapplicable to the holiest of God's servants, who are all far from fulfilling the law, and are encompassed with a multitude of transgressions (Rom. 10:5ff.). But when these are superseded by the evangelical promises, which proclaim the gratuitous remission of sins, the consequence is, that not only our persons, but also our works, are accepted by God; and not accepted only, but followed by those blessings, which were due by the covenant to the observance of the law. I grant, therefore, that the works of believers are rewarded by those things which the Lord has promised in his law to the followers of righteousness and holiness; but in this retribution it is always necessary to consider the cause, which conciliates such favor to those works.

Now, this we perceive to be threefold: The first is that God, averting his eyes from the actions of his servants, which are invariably more deserving of censure than of praise, receives and embraces them in Christ, and by the intervention of faith alone reconciles them to himself without the assistance of works. The second is that, in his paternal benignity and indulgence, he overlooks the intrinsic worth of these works, and exalts them to such honor that he esteems them of some degree of value. The third cause is that he pardons these works as he receives them, not imputing the imperfection with which they are all so defiled, that they might otherwise be accounted rather sins than virtues. Hence it appears how great has been the delusion of the sophists, who thought that they had dexterously avoided all absurdities by saying that works are sufficient to merit salvation, not on account of their own intrinsic goodness, but by reason of the covenant, because the Lord in his mercy has estimated them so highly. But at the same time, they had not observed how far the works, which they styled *meritorious*, fell short of the condition of the promise; unless they were preceded by justification founded on faith alone, and by remission of sins, by which even good works require to be purified from blemishes. Therefore, of the three causes of the Divine goodness, in consequence of which the works of believers are accepted, they only noticed one, and suppressed two others, and those the principal.

IV. Considering God's Acceptance of Cornelius

They allege the declaration of Peter, which Luke recites in the Acts: "Of a truth I perceive that God is no respecter of persons; but in every nation he that works righteousness is accepted with him" (Acts 10:34-35). And hence they conclude, what they think admits of no doubt, that if a man by rectitude of conduct conciliate to himself the favor of God, the grace of God is not the sole cause of his salvation. Moreover, that God of his own mercy assists a sinner in such a manner, as to be influenced to the exercise of mercy by his works.

But we cannot by any means reconcile the Scriptures with themselves, unless we observe a twofold acceptance of man with God. For God finds nothing in man, in his native condition, to incline him to mercy, but mere misery. If, then, it is evident that man is entirely destitute of all good, and full of every kind of evil, when he is first received by God, by what good qualities shall we pronounce him entitled to the heavenly calling? Let us reject, therefore, all vain imagination of merits, where God so evidently displays his unmerited clemency. The declaration of the angel to Cornelius in the same passage, "Your prayers and your alms are come up for a memorial before God," they most wickedly pervert to prove that the practice of good works prepares a man to receive the grace of God. For Cornelius must have been already illuminated with the Spirit of wisdom, since he was endued with the fear of God, which is true wisdom; and he must have been sanctified by the same Spirit, since he was a follower of righteousness, which the apostle represents as one of the Spirit's most certain fruits (Gal. 5:5). It was from the grace of God, then, that he derived all these things in which he is said to have pleased him; so far was he from preparing himself to receive it by the exercise of his own powers.

There cannot indeed be adduced a single syllable of the Scripture, which is not in harmony with this doctrine; that there is no other cause for God's reception of man into his love than his knowledge that man, if abandoned by him, would be utterly lost; and because it is not his will to abandon him to perdition, he displays his mercy in his deliverance. Now, we see that this acceptance is irrespective of the righteousness of man, but is an unequivocal proof of the Divine goodness towards miserable sinners, who are infinitely unworthy of so great a favor.

V. God's Acceptance Based on His Own Mercy

After the Lord has recovered a man from the abyss of perdition, and separated him to himself by the grace of adoption,—because he has regenerated him, and raised him to a new life, he now receives and embraces him as a new creature with the gifts of his Spirit. This is the acceptance mentioned by Peter, in which even the works of believers after their vocation are approved by God; for the Lord cannot but love and accept those good effects which are produced in them by his Spirit.

But it must always be remembered that they are accepted by God in consequence of their works, only because, for their sakes and the favor which he bears to them, he deigns to accept whatever goodness he has liberally communicated to their works. For whence proceeds the goodness of their works, but from the Lord's determination to adorn with true purity those whom he has chosen as vessels of honor? And how is it that they are accounted good, as though they were free from all imperfection, except from the mercy of their Father, who pardons the blemishes which adhere to them? In a word, Peter intends nothing else in this passage, but that God accepts and loves his children, in whom he beholds the marks and lineaments of his own countenance. For we have elsewhere shown that regeneration is a reparation of the Divine image in us. Wherever the Lord contemplates his own likeness, he justly both loves and honors it. The life of his children, therefore, being devoted to holiness and righteousness, is truly represented as pleasing to him. But as the faithful, while they are surrounded with mortal flesh, are still sinners, and all their works are imperfect, and tainted with the vices of the flesh, he cannot be propitious either to their persons or to their works, without regarding them in Christ rather than in themselves. It is in this sense that those passages must be understood, which declare God to be merciful and compassionate to the followers of righteousness.

Moses said to the Israelites, "The Lord your God, which keeps covenant and mercy with them that love him and keep his commandments to a thousand generations" (Deut. 7:9)—a sentence which was afterwards in frequent use among that people. Thus Solomon, in his solemn prayer: "Lord God of Israel, who keeps covenant and mercy with your servants that walk before you with all their heart" (1 Kings 8:23). The same language is also repeated by Nehemiah (Neh. 1:5). For as, in all the covenants of his mercy the Lord stipulates with his servants for integrity and sanctity in their lives, that his goodness may not become an object of contempt, and that no man infected with a vain confidence in his mercy (Deut. 29:19-20), may bless himself in his mind while walking in the depravity of his heart, so he designs by these means to confine to their duty all that are admitted to the participation of his covenant. Yet, nevertheless, the covenant is originally constituted and perpetually remains altogether gratuitous. For this reason, David, though he declares that he had been rewarded for the purity of his hands, does not overlook that original source which I have mentioned: "He delivered me, because he delighted in me" (2 Sam. 22:20-21); where he commends the goodness of his cause, so as not to derogate from the gratuitous mercy which precedes all the gifts that originate from it.

VI. Legal vs. Evangelical Promises

And here it will be useful to remark, by the way, what difference there is between such forms of expression and the legal promises. By legal promises I intend, not all those which are contained in the books of Moses,—since in those books there likewise occur many evangelical ones,—but such as properly pertain to the ministry of the law. Such promises, by whatever appellation they may be distinguished, proclaim that a reward is ready to be bestowed, on condition that we perform what is commanded. But when it is said that "the Lord keeps covenant and mercy with them that love him," this rather designates the characters of his servants, who have faithfully received his covenant, than expresses the causes of his beneficence to them. Now, this is the way to prove it.

As the Lord favors us with the hope of eternal life, in order that he may be loved, reverenced, and worshipped by us, therefore all the promises of mercy contained in the Scriptures are justly directed to this end, that we may revere and worship the Author of our blessings. Whenever, therefore, we hear of his beneficence to them who observe his laws, let us remember that the children of God are designated by the duty in which they ought always to be found; and that we are adopted as his children, in order that we may venerate him as our Father. Therefore, that we may not renounce the privilege of our adoption, we ought to aim at that which is the design of our vocation. On the other hand, however, we may be assured that the accomplishment of God's mercy is independent of the works of believers; but that he fulfils the promise of salvation to them whose vocation is followed by a correspondent rectitude of life, because in them who are directed by his Spirit to good works, he recognizes the genuine characters of his children.

To this must be referred what is said of the citizens of the Church: "Lord, who shall abide in your tabernacle? who shall dwell in thy holy hill? He that walks uprightly, and works righteousness," &c. (Psa. 15:1-2). And in Isaiah: "Who shall dwell with the devouring fire? He that walks righteously, and speaks uprightly," &c. (Isa. 33:14-15). For these passages describe, not the foundation which supports the faithful before God, but the manner in which their most merciful Father introduces them into communion with him, and preserves and confirms them in it. For as he detests sin, and loves righteousness, those whom he unites to him he purifies by his Spirit, in order to conform them to himself and his kingdom. Therefore, if it be inquired what is the first cause which gives the saints an entrance into the kingdom of God, and which makes their continuance in it permanent, the answer is ready. Because the Lord in his mercy has once adopted and perpetually defends them. But if the question relate to the manner in which he does this, it will then be necessary to advert to regeneration and its fruits, which are enumerated in the psalm that we have just quoted.

VII. On Distinguishing Good Works as "Righteousness"
But there appears to be much greater difficulty in those places which dignify good works with the title of *righteousness*, and assert that a man is justified by them. Of the former kind there are many, where the observance of the commands is

denominated *justification* or *righteousness*. An example of the other kind we find in Moses: "And it shall be our righteousness, if we observe to do all these commandments" (Deut. 6:25). If it be objected that this is a legal promise, which, having an impossible condition annexed to it, proves nothing,—there are other passages which will not admit of a similar reply; such as, "In case you shall deliver him the pledge, &c., it shall be righteousness unto you before the Lord" (Deut. 24:13). Similar to this is what the Psalmist says, that the zeal of Phinehas in avenging the disgrace of Israel, "was counted unto him for righteousness" (Psa. 106:30-31).

Therefore the Pharisees of our day suppose that these passages afford ample ground for their clamor against us. For when we say that if the righteousness of faith be established, there is an end of justification by works,—they argue, in the same manner, that if righteousness be by works, then it is not true that we are justified by faith alone. Though I grant that the precepts of the law are termed *righteousness*, there is nothing surprising in this; for they are so in reality. The reader, however, ought to be apprized that the Hebrew word *khuqqim* (commandments) is not well translated by the Greek word *dikaiōmata*, (righteousness). But I readily relinquish all controversy respecting the word. Nor do we deny that the Divine law contains perfect righteousness. For although, being under an obligation to fulfil all its precepts, we should, even after a perfect obedience to it, only be unprofitable servants,— yet since the Lord has honored the observance of it with the title of *righteousness*, we would not detract from what he has given.

We freely acknowledge, therefore, that the perfect obedience of the law is righteousness, and that the observance of every particular command is a part of righteousness; since complete righteousness consists of all the parts. But we deny that such a kind of righteousness anywhere exists. And therefore we reject the righteousness of the law; not that it is of itself defective and mutilated, but because, on account of the debility of our flesh (Rom. 8:3), it is nowhere to be found. It may be said that the Scripture not only calls the Divine precepts *righteousnesses*, but gives this appellation also to the works of the saints. As where it relates of Zacharias and his wife, that "they were both righteous before God, walking in all his commandments" (Luke 1:6); certainly, when it speaks thus, it estimates their works rather according to the nature of the law, than according to the actual condition of the persons.

Here it is necessary to repeat the observation which I have just made, that no rule is to be drawn from the incautiousness of the Greek translator. But as Luke has not thought proper to alter the common version, neither will I contend for it. Those things which are commanded in the law, God has enjoined upon man as necessary to righteousness; but that righteousness we do not fulfil without observing the whole law, which is broken by every act of transgression. Since the law, therefore, only prescribes a righteousness, if we contemplate the law itself, all its distinct commands are parts of righteousness; if we consider men, by whom they are performed, they cannot obtain the praise of righteousness from one act, while they are transgressors in many, and while that same act is partly vicious by reason of its imperfection.

VIII. The Value of Works and the Righteousness of Faith

But I proceed to the second class of texts in which the principal difficulty lies. Paul urges nothing more forcible in proof of justification by faith than what is stated respecting Abraham—

Harmony Between the Promises

that he "believed God, and it was counted unto him for righteousness" (Rom. 4:3; Gal. 3:6). Since the action of Phinehas, therefore, is said to have been "counted unto him for righteousness" (Psa. 106:31), we may also use the same argument concerning works, which Paul insists on respecting faith. Therefore our adversaries, as though they had established the point, determine that we are justified neither without faith, nor by faith alone; and that our righteousness is completed by works.

Therefore I conjure believers, if they know that the true rule of righteousness is to be sought in the Scripture alone, to accompany me in a serious and solemn examination how the Scripture may be properly reconciled with itself without any sophistry. Paul, knowing the righteousness of faith to be the refuge of those who are destitute of any righteousness of their own, boldly infers that all who are justified by faith, are excluded from the righteousness of works. It being likewise evident, on the other hand, that this is common to all believers, he with equal confidence concludes that no man is justified by works, but rather, on the contrary, that we are justified independently of all works.

But it is one thing to dispute concerning the intrinsic value of works, and another, to argue respecting the place they ought to hold after the establishment of the righteousness of faith. If we are to determine the value of works by their own worthiness, we say that they are unworthy to appear in the sight of God; that there is nothing in our works of which we can glory before God; and consequently, that being divested of all assistance from works, we are justified by faith alone. Now, we describe this righteousness in the following manner: that a sinner, being admitted to communion with Christ, is by his grace reconciled to God; while, being purified by his blood, he obtains remission of sins, and being clothed with his righteousness, as if it were his own, he stands secure before the heavenly tribunal. Where remission of sins has been previously received, the good works which succeed are estimated far beyond their intrinsic merit. For all their imperfections are covered by the perfection of Christ, and all their blemishes are removed by his purity, that they may not be scrutinized by the Divine judgment. The guilt, therefore, of all transgressions, by which men are prevented from offering anything acceptable, to God being obliterated, and the imperfection, which universally deforms even the good works of believers, being buried in oblivion, their works are accounted righteous, or, which is the same thing, are imputed for righteousness.

IX. The Righteousness of Faith Fortified

Now, if any one urge this to me as an objection, to oppose the righteousness of faith, I will first ask him, whether a man is reputed righteous on account of one or two holy works, who is in the other actions of his life a transgressor of the law. This would be too absurd to be pretended. I shall next inquire, if he is reputed righteous on account of many good works, while he is found guilty of any instance of transgression. This, likewise, my adversary will not presume to maintain, in opposition to the sanction of the law, which denounces a curse on all those who do not fulfil every one of its precepts (Deut. 27:26). I will further inquire, if there is any work which does not deserve the charge of impurity or imperfection (Job 4:18; 15:15; 25:5). But how could this be possible before those eyes, in which the stars are not sufficiently pure, nor the angels sufficiently righteous? Thus he will be compelled to concede that there is not a good work to be found, which is not too much polluted, both by its own imperfection and by the transgressions with which it is attended, to have any claim to the honorable appellation of righteousness.

Now, if it be evidently in consequence of justification by faith that works, otherwise impure and imperfect, unworthy of the sight of God, and much more of his approbation, are imputed for righteousness,—why do they attempt, by boasting of the righteousness of works, to destroy the righteousness of faith from which all righteousness of works proceeds? But do they wish to produce a viperous offspring to destroy the parent? For such is the true tendency of this impious doctrine. They cannot deny that justification by faith is the beginning, foundation, cause, motive, and substance of the righteousness of works; yet they conclude that a man is not justified by faith because good works also are imputed for righteousness.

Let us therefore leave these impertinences, and acknowledge the real state of the case. If all the righteousness which can be attributed to works depends on justification by faith, the latter is not only not diminished, but, on the contrary, is confirmed by it; since its influence appears the more extensive. But let us not suppose that works, subsequent to gratuitous justification, are so highly esteemed, that they succeed to the office of justifying men, or divide that office with faith. For unless justification by faith remain always unimpaired, the impurity of their works will be detected. Nor is there any absurdity in saying, that a man is so justified by faith, that he is not only righteous himself, but that even his works are accounted righteous beyond what they deserve.

X. God Does Not Accept Partial, Imperfect Righteousness

In this way we will admit, not only a partial righteousness of works, which our opponents maintain, but such as is approved by God, as though it were perfect and complete. A remembrance of the foundation on which it stands will solve every difficulty. For no work is ever acceptable till it be received with pardon. Now, whence proceeds pardon, but from God's beholding us and all our actions in Christ? When we are grafted into Christ, therefore, as our persons appear righteous before God, because our iniquities are covered by his righteousness, so our works are accounted righteous, because the sinfulness otherwise belonging to them is not imputed, being all buried in the purity of Christ. So we may justly assert that not only our persons, but even our works, are justified by faith alone.

Now, if this righteousness of works, whatever be its nature, is consequent and dependent on faith and gratuitous justification, it ought to be included under it, and subordinated to it, as an effect to its cause; so far is it from deserving to be exalted, either to destroy or to obscure the righteousness of faith. Thus Paul, to evince that our blessedness depends on the mercy of God, and not on our works, chiefly urges this declaration of David: "Blessed are they whose iniquities are forgiven, and whose sins are covered. Blessed is the man to whom the Lord will not impute sin" (Rom. 4:7-8; Psa. 32:1-2). If, in opposition to this, the numerous passages be adduced where blessedness seems to be attributed to works; such as, "Blessed is the man that fears the Lord (Psa. 112:1); that has mercy on the poor (Prov. 14:21); that walks not in the counsel of the ungodly (Psa. 1:1); that endures temptation" (Jas. 1:12); "Blessed are they that keep judgment (Psa. 106:3); the undefiled (Psa. 119:1), the poor in spirit, the meek, the merciful," &c. (Matt. 5:3, 5, 7);

they will not at all weaken the truth of what is advanced by Paul. For since no man ever attains all these characters, so as thereby to gain the Divine approbation, it appears that men are always miserable till they are delivered from misery by the pardon of their sins.

Since all the beatitudes celebrated in the Scriptures are of no avail, and no man can derive any benefit from them till he has obtained blessedness by the remission of his sins, which then makes room for the other beatitudes, it follows that this is not merely the noblest and principal, but the only blessedness; unless, indeed, we suppose it to be diminished by those which are dependent on it. Now, we have much less reason to be disturbed by the appellation of *righteous*, which is generally given to believers. I acknowledge that they are denominated *righteous* from the sanctity of their lives; but as they rather devote themselves to the pursuit of righteousness than actually attain to righteousness itself, it is proper that this righteousness, such as it is, should be subordinate to justification by faith, from which it derives its origin.

XI. Are James and Paul in Disagreement with One Another?

But our adversaries say that we have yet more difficulty with James, since he contradicts us in express terms. For he teaches that "Abraham was justified by works," and that we are all "justified by works, and not by faith only" (Jas. 2:21, 24). What then? Will they draw Paul into a controversy with James? If they consider James as a minister of Christ, his declarations must be understood in some sense not at variance with Christ when speaking by the mouth of Paul. The Spirit asserts, by the mouth of Paul, that Abraham obtained righteousness by faith, not by works; we likewise teach, that we are all justified by faith without the works of the law. The same Spirit affirms by James, that both Abraham's righteousness and ours consists in works, and not in faith only. That the Spirit is not inconsistent with himself is a certain truth. But what harmony can there be between these two apparently opposite assertions?

Our adversaries would be satisfied, if they could totally subvert the righteousness of faith, which we wish to be firmly established; but to afford tranquility to the disturbed conscience, they feel very little concern. Hence we perceive that they oppose the doctrine of justification by faith, but at the same time fix no certain rule of righteousness, by which the conscience may be satisfied. Let them triumph then as they please, if they can boast no other victory but that of having removed all certainty of righteousness. And this miserable victory, indeed, they will obtain, where, after having extinguished the light of truth, they are permitted by the Lord to spread the shades of error. But, wherever the truth of God remains, they will not prevail. I deny, therefore, that the assertion of James, which they hold up against us as an impenetrable shield, affords them the least support.

To evince this, we shall first examine the scope of the apostle, and then remark wherein they are deceived. Because there were many persons at that time, and the Church is perpetually infested with similar characters, who, by neglecting and omitting the proper duties of believers, manifestly betrayed their real infidelity, while they continued to glory in the false pretense of faith, James here exposes the foolish confidence of such persons. It is not his design, then, to diminish, in any respect, the virtue of true faith, but to show the folly of these triflers, who were content with arrogating to themselves the vain image of it, and securely abandoned themselves to every vice.

This statement being premised, it will be easy to discover where lies the error of our adversaries. For they fall into two fallacies; one respecting the word "faith," the other respecting the word "justification." When the apostle gives the appellation of *faith* to a vain notion, widely different from true faith, it is a concession which derogates nothing from the argument; this he shows from the beginning in these words: "What does it profit, my brethren, though a man say he has faith, and have not works" (Jas. 2:14)? He does not say, 'If anyone have faith without works;' but, 'If any one boast of having it.' He speaks still more plainly just after, where he ridicules it by representing it as worse than the knowledge of devils; and lastly, when he calls it dead. But his meaning may be sufficiently understood from the definition he gives: "You believe," says he, "that there is one God." Indeed, if nothing be contained in this creed but a belief of the Divine existence, it is not at all surprising that it is inadequate to justification. And we must not suppose this denial to be derogatory to Christian faith, the nature of which is widely different. For how does true faith justify, but by uniting us to Christ, that, being made one with him, we may participate his righteousness? It does not, therefore, justify us, by attaining a knowledge of God's existence, but by a reliance on the certainty of his mercy.

XII. Paul and James on *Justification*

But we shall not have ascertained the whole scope of the apostle till we have exposed the other fallacy; for he attributes justification partly to works. If we wish to make James consistent with the rest of the Scriptures, and even with himself, we must understand the word "justify" in a different signification from that in which it is used by Paul. For we are

JUSTIFICATION BY FAITH

said by Paul to be justified, when the memory of our unrighteousness is obliterated, and we are accounted righteous. If James had alluded to this, it would have been preposterous for him to make that quotation from Moses: "Abraham believed God," &c. (Jas. 2:21-23; cf. Gen. 15:6). For, he introduces it in the following manner: Abraham obtained righteousness by works, because he hesitated not to sacrifice his son at the command of God. And thus was the Scripture fulfilled, which says, "Abraham believed God, and it was imputed unto him for righteousness." If an effect antecedent to its cause be an absurdity, either Moses falsely asserts in that place that Abraham's faith was imputed to him for righteousness, or Abraham did not obtain righteousness by his obedience, displayed in the oblation of his son. Abraham was justified by faith, while Ishmael, who arrived at adolescence before the birth of Isaac, was not yet conceived. How, then, can we ascribe his justification to an act of obedience performed so long after? Wherefore, either James improperly inverted the order of events (which it is unlawful to imagine), or, by saying that Abraham was justified, he did not mean that the patriarch deserved to be accounted righteous.

What, then, was his meaning? He evidently appears to speak of a declaration of righteousness before men, and not of an imputation of it in the sight of God; as though he had said, "They who are justified by true faith prove their justification, not by a barren and imaginary resemblance of faith, but by obedience and good works." In a word, he is not disputing concerning the method of justification, but requiring of believers a righteousness manifested in good works. And as Paul contends for justification independent of works, so James will not allow those to be accounted righteous, who are destitute of good works. The consideration of this object will extricate us from every difficulty. For the principal mistake of our adversaries consists in supposing that James describes the method of justification, while he only endeavors to destroy the corrupt security of those who make vain pretenses to faith, in order to excuse their contempt of good works. Into whatever forms, therefore, they pervert the words of James, they will extort nothing but these two truths—that a vain notion of faith cannot justify; and that the faithful, not content with such an imagination, manifest their righteousness by their good works.

XIII. Paul's Argument from Romans 2:13

Nor can they derive the least support from a similar passage which they cite from Paul that, "Not the hearers of the law, but the doers of the law shall be justified" (Rom. 2:13). I have no wish to evade it by the explanation of Ambrose, that this is spoken because faith in Christ is the fulfilling of the law. For this I conceive to be a mere subterfuge, which is totally unnecessary. The apostle in that place is demolishing the foolish confidence of the Jews, who boasted of possessing the exclusive knowledge of the law, whilst at the same time they were the greatest despisers of it. To prevent such great self-complacence on account of a mere acquaintance with the law, he admonishes them, that if righteousness be sought by the law, it is requisite not only to know but to observe it.

We certainly do not question that the righteousness of the law consists in works, nor that this righteousness consists in the worthiness and merit of works. But still it cannot be proved that we are justified by works, unless some person be produced who has fulfilled the law. That Paul had no other meaning is sufficiently evident from the context. After having condemned the Gentiles and Jews indiscriminately for unrighteousness, he proceeds particularly to inform us, that "as many as have sinned without law shall also perish without law;" which refers to the Gentiles; and that "as many as have sinned in the law shall be judged by the law;" which belongs to the Jews. Moreover, because they shut their eyes against their transgressions, and gloried in their mere possession of the law, he adds, what is exceedingly applicable, that the law was not given that men might be justified merely by hearing its voice, but by obeying it; as though he had said, 'Do you seek righteousness by the law? Plead not your having heard it, which of itself is a very small advantage, but produce works as an evidence that the law has not been given to you in vain.' Since in this respect they were all deficient, they were consequently deprived of their glorying in the law. The meaning of Paul therefore, rather furnishes an opposite argument: Legal righteousness consists in perfect works; no man can boast of having satisfied the law by his works; therefore there is no righteousness by the law.

XIV. Can We Appeal to Our Own Righteousness?

Our adversaries proceed to adduce those passages in which the faithful boldly offer their righteousness to the examination of Divine justice, and desire to be judged according to it. Such are the following: "Judge me, O Lord, according to my righteousness, and according to mine integrity that is in me" (Psa. 7:8). Again: "Hear the right, O Lord, you have proved mine heart; you have visited me in the night; you have tried me, and shall find nothing" (Psa. 17:1, 3). Again: "I have kept the ways of the Lord, and have not wickedly departed from my God. I was also upright before him, and I kept myself from mine iniquity. Therefore has the Lord recompensed me according to my righteousness, according to the cleanness of my hands" (Psa. 18:21, 23, 24). Again: "Judge me, O Lord, for I have walked in my integrity. I have not sat with vain persons; neither will I go in with dissemblers. Gather not my soul with sinners, nor my life with bloody men; in whose hands is mischief, and their right hand is full of bribes. But as for me, I will walk in mine integrity" (Psa. 26:1, 4, 9-11). I have already spoken of the confidence which the saints appear to derive from their works. The passages now adduced will form no objection to our doctrine, when they are explained according to the occasion of them.

Now, this is twofold. For believers who have expressed themselves in this manner have no wish to submit to a general examination to be condemned or absolved according to the whole tenor of their lives, but they bring forward a particular cause to be judged; and they attribute righteousness to themselves, not with reference to the Divine perfection, but in comparison with men of impious and abandoned characters. In the first place, in order to a man's being justified, it is requisite that he should have, not only a good cause in some particular instance, but a perpetual consistency of righteousness through life. But the saints, when they implore the judgment of God in approbation of their innocence, do not present themselves as free from every charge, and absolutely guiltless; but having fixed their dependence on his goodness alone, and confiding in his readiness to avenge the poor who are unlawfully and unjustly afflicted, they supplicate his regard to the cause in which the innocent are oppressed. But when they place themselves and their adversaries before the Divine tribunal, they boast not an innocence, which, on a severe examination, would be found correspondent to the purity of God; but knowing that their

JUSTIFICATION BY FAITH

sincerity, justice, simplicity, and purity, are pleasing and acceptable to God, in comparison with the malice, wickedness, fraud, and iniquity of their enemies, they are not afraid to invoke Him to judge between them.

Thus, when David said to Saul, "The Lord render to every man his righteousness and his faithfulness" (1 Sam. 26:23), he did not mean that the Lord should examine every individual by himself, and reward him according to his merits; but he called the Lord to witness the greatness of his innocence in comparison with the iniquity of Saul. Nor did Paul, when he gloried in having "the testimony of" his "conscience" that he had conducted himself in the Church "with simplicity and godly sincerity" (2 Cor. 1:12), intend to rely on this before God; but the calumnies of the impious constrained him to oppose all their slanderous aspersions by asserting his fidelity and probity, which he knew to be acceptable to the Divine goodness. For we know what he says in another place: "I am conscious to myself of nothing; yet am I not hereby justified" (1 Cor. 4:4). Because, indeed, he was certain that the judgment of God far transcended the narrow comprehension of man. However, therefore, the pious may vindicate their innocence against the hypocrisy of the impious by invoking God to be their witness and judge, yet in their concerns with God alone, they all with one voice exclaim, "If you, Lord, should mark iniquities, O Lord, who shall stand" (Psa. 130:3)? Again: "Enter not into judgment with your servant, for in your sight shall no man living be justified" (Psa. 143:2). And, diffident of their own works, they gladly sing, "Your loving-kindness is better than life" (Psa. 63:3).

XV. Righteousness as a Way of Life

There are likewise other passages, similar to the preceding, on which some person may yet insist. Solomon says, "The just man walks in his integrity" (Prov. 20:7). Again: "In the way of righteousness there is life; and in the pathway thereof there is no death" (Prov. 12:28). Thus also Ezekiel declares that he who "does that which is lawful and right, shall surely live" (Ezek. 33:14-15). We neither deny nor obscure any of these. But let one of the sons of Adam produce such an integrity. If no one can, they must either perish from the presence of God, or flee to the asylum of mercy.

Nor do we deny that to believers their integrity, however imperfect, is a step toward immortality. But what is the cause of this, unless it be that when the Lord has admitted any persons into the covenant of his grace, he does not scrutinize their works according to their intrinsic merit, but embraces them with paternal benignity? By this we mean, not merely what is taught by the schoolmen, "that works receive their value from the grace which accepts them;" for they suppose that works, otherwise inadequate to the attainment of salvation by the legal covenant, are rendered sufficient for this by the Divine acceptance of them. But I assert that they are so defiled, both by other transgressions and by their own blemishes, that they are of no value at all, except as the Lord pardons both; and this is no other than bestowing on a man gratuitous righteousness.

It is irrelevant to this subject to allege those prayers of the apostle, in which he desires such perfection for believers, that they may be unblamable and irreprovable in the day of Christ (1 Thes. 3:13, etc.). These passages, indeed, the Celestines formerly perverted, in order to prove a perfection of righteousness in the present life. We think it sufficient briefly to reply with Augustine, "that all the pious ought, indeed, to aspire to this object, to appear one day immaculate and guiltless before the presence of God; but since the highest excellency in this life is nothing more than a progress towards perfection, we shall never attain it, till, being divested at once of mortality and sin, we shall fully adhere to the Lord." Nevertheless, I shall not pertinaciously contend with any person who chooses to attribute to the saints the character of perfection, provided he also defines it in the words of Augustine himself who says, "When we denominate the virtue of the saints perfect, to this perfection itself belongs the acknowledgment of imperfection, both in truth and in humility."[1]

---

[1] Augustine, *Against Two Pelagian Letters to Pope Boniface*, vol. 3, c. 7.

8

Justification from Works Not to Be Inferred from the Promise of a Reward

I. What is Meant by the Term "Working"

Let us now proceed to those passages which affirm that "God will render to every man according to his deeds" (Rom. 2:6; Matt. 16:27); that "every one may receive the things done in his body, according to that he has done, whether it be good or bad" (2 Cor. 5:10). "Tribulation and anguish upon every soul that does evil; but glory, honor, and peace, to every man that works good" (Rom. 2:9-10). And, "All shall come forth; they that have done good, unto the resurrection of life; and they that have done evil, unto the resurrection of damnation" (John 5:29). "Come, you blessed of my Father; for I was a hungered, and you gave me meat: I was thirsty, and you gave me drink," &c. (Matt. 25:34-36). And with these let us also connect those which represent eternal life as the reward of works, such as the following: "The recompense of a man's hands shall be rendered unto him" (Prov. 12:14). "He that fears the commandment shall be rewarded" (Prov. 13:13). "Rejoice and be exceeding glad; for great is your reward in heaven" (Matt. 5:12; Luke 6:23).

"Everyone shall receive his own reward, according to his own labor" (1 Cor. 3:8).

The declaration that "God will render to every one according to his works" is easily explained. For that phrase indicates the order of events, rather than the cause of them. But it is beyond all doubt that the Lord proceeds to the consummation of our salvation by these several gradations of mercy: "Whom he has predestinated, them he calls; whom he has called, he justifies; and whom he has justified, he finally glorifies" (Rom. 8:30). Though he receives his children into eternal life, therefore, of his mere mercy, yet since he conducts them to the possession of it through a course of good works, that he may fulfil his work in them in the order he has appointed, we need not wonder if they are said to be rewarded according to their works by which they are undoubtedly prepared to receive the crown of immortality. And for this reason, they are properly said to "work out their own salvation" (Phil. 2:12), while devoting themselves to good works, they aspire to eternal life; just as in another place they are commanded to "labor for the meat which perishes not," when they obtain eternal life by believing in Christ; and yet it is immediately added, "which the Son of man shall give unto you" (John 6:27).

Whence it appears that the word *work* is not opposed to grace, but refers to human endeavors; and therefore it does not follow, either that believers are the authors of their own salvation, or that salvation proceeds from their works. But as soon as they are introduced, by the knowledge of the gospel and the illumination of the Holy Spirit, into communion with Christ, eternal life is begun in them. Now, "the good work which" God "has begun in" them, "he will perform until the day of Jesus Christ" (Phil. 1:6). And it is performed when they prove themselves to be the genuine children of God by their resemblance to their heavenly Father in righteousness and holiness.

II. The Works of Believers Do Not Cause Their Salvation

We have no reason to infer from the term *reward*, that good works are the cause of salvation. First, let this truth be established in our minds, that the kingdom of heaven is not the stipend of servants, but the inheritance of children, which will be enjoyed only by those whom the Lord adopts as his children, and for no other cause than on account of this adoption. "For the son of the bond-woman shall not be heir with the son of the free woman" (Gal. 4:30). And, therefore, in the same passages in which the Holy Spirit promises eternal life as the reward of works, by expressly denominating it "an inheritance," he proves it to proceed from another cause. Thus Christ enumerates the works which he compensates by the reward of heaven, when he calls the elect to the possession of it; but at the same time adds, that it is to be enjoyed by right of inheritance (Matt. 25:34). So Paul encourages servants who faithfully discharge their duty to hope for a reward from the Lord; but at the same time calls it "the reward of the inheritance" (Col. 3:24). We see how they, almost in express terms, caution us against attributing eternal life to works, instead of ascribing it to Divine adoption.

Why, then, it may be asked, do they at the same time make mention of works? This question shall be elucidated by one example from the Scripture. Before the nativity of Isaac, there had been promised to Abraham a seed in whom all the nations of the earth were to be blessed, a multiplication of his posterity, which would equal the stars of heaven and the sands of the sea, and other similar blessings (Gen. 12:2-3; 13:16; 15:5). Many years after, in consequence of a Divine command, Abraham prepares to sacrifice his son. After this act of obedience, he receives this promise:

> By myself have I sworn, says the Lord, for because you have done this thing, and have not withheld your son, your only son; that in blessing I will bless you, and in multiplying I will multiply your seed as the stars of the heaven, and as the sand which is upon the sea-shore; and your seed shall possess the gate of his enemies; and in your seed shall all the nations of the earth be blessed; because you have obeyed my voice (Gen. 22:16-18).

What? did Abraham by his obedience merit that blessing which had been promised him before the command was delivered? Here, then, it appears, beyond all doubt, that the Lord rewards the works of believers with those blessings which he had already given them before their works were thought of, and while he had no reason for his beneficence, but his own mercy.

III. On Eternal Life as a "Reward"

Nor does the Lord deceive or trifle with us when he says that he will requite works with what he had freely given previously to the performance of them. For since it is his pleasure that we be employed in good works, while aspiring after the manifestation or enjoyment of those things which he has promised, and that they constitute the road in which we should travel to endeavor to attain the blessed hope proposed to us in heaven, therefore the fruit of the promises, to the perfection of which fruit those works conduct us, is justly assigned to them.

Promise of a Reward

The apostle beautifully expressed both those ideas when he said that the Colossians applied themselves to the duties of charity, "for the hope which was laid up for them in heaven, whereof they heard before in the word, of the truth of the gospel" (Col. 1:4-5). For his assertion, that they knew from the gospel, that there was hope laid up for them in heaven, is equivalent to a declaration that it depended not on any works, but on Christ alone; which perfectly accords with the observation of Peter, that believers "are kept by the power of God through faith unto salvation, ready to be revealed in the last time" (1 Pet. 1:5). When it is said that they must labor for it, it implies that, in order to attain to it, believers have a race to run, which terminates only with their lives.

But that we might not suppose the reward promised us by the Lord to be regulated according to the proportion of merit, he proposes a parable, in which he has represented himself under the character of a householder, who employs all the persons he meets in the cultivation of his vineyard; some he hires at the first hour of the day, others at the second, others at the third, and some even at the eleventh hour; in the evening he pays them all the same wages (Matt. 20:1ff.). A brief and just explanation of this parable is given by the ancient writer, whoever he was, of the treatise, *On the Calling of the Gentiles*, which bears the name of Ambrose. I shall adopt his words in preference to my own.

> By the example of this comparison (says he), the Lord has shown a variety of manifold vocation pertaining to the same grace. They who, having been admitted into the vineyard at the eleventh hour, are placed on an equality with them who had labored the whole day,

represent the state of those whom, to magnify the excellence of grace, God, in his mercy, has rewarded in the decline of the day, and at the conclusion of life; not paying them the wages due to their labor, but sending down the riches of his goodness, in copious effusions, on them whom he has chosen without works; that even they who have labored the most, and have received no more than the last, may understand theirs to be a reward of grace, not of works.

Lastly, it is also worthy of being observed that in those places where eternal life is called a reward of works, it is not to be understood simply of that communion which we have with God, as the prelude to a happy immortality, when he embraces us in Christ with paternal benevolence, but of the possession or fruition of ultimate blessedness, as the very words of Christ import—"in the world to come, eternal life" (Mark 10:30). And in another place, "Come, inherit the kingdom," &c. (Matt. 25:34). For the same reason, Paul applies the term *adoption* to the revelation of adoption, which shall be made in the resurrection; and afterwards explains it to be "the redemption of our body" (Rom. 8:23). Otherwise, as alienation from God is eternal death, so when a man is received into the favor of God so as to enjoy communion with him and become united to him, he is translated from death to life; which is solely the fruit of adoption. And if they insist, with their accustomed pertinacity, on the reward of works, we may retort against them that passage of Peter, where eternal life is called "the end (or reward) of faith" (1 Pet. 1:9).

IV. Holiness as the Way of Eternal Life

Let us not, therefore, imagine that the Holy Spirit by these promises commends the worthiness of our works, as though they merited such a reward. For the Scripture leaves us nothing that can exalt us in the Divine presence. Its whole tendency is rather to repress our arrogance, and to inspire us with humility, dejection, and contrition. But such promises assist our weakness, which otherwise would immediately slide and fall, if it did not sustain itself by this expectation, and alleviate its sorrows by this consolation.

First, let everyone reflect how difficult it is for a man to relinquish and renounce not only all that belong to him, but even himself. And yet this is the first lesson which Christ teaches his disciples, that is to say, all the pious. Afterwards he gives them such tuition during the remainder of their lives, under the discipline of the cross, that their hearts may not fix either their desires or their dependence on present advantages. In short, he generally manages them in such a manner, that whithersoever they turn their views throughout the world, nothing but despair presents itself to them on every side; so that Paul says, "If in this life only we have hope in Christ, we are of all men most miserable" (1 Cor. 15:19). To preserve them from sinking under these afflictions, they have the presence of the Lord, who encourages them to raise their heads higher, and to extend their views further, by assurances that they will find in him that blessedness which they cannot see in the world. This blessedness he calls a *reward*, a *recompense*; not attributing any merit to their works, but signifying that it is a compensation for their oppressions, sufferings, and disgrace. Wherefore there is no objection against our following the example of the Scripture in calling eternal life a *reward*, since in that state the Lord receives his people from labor into rest; from affliction into prosperity and happiness; from sorrow into joy; from poverty into affluence; from ignominy into glory; and commutes all the evils which they have endured for blessings of superior magnitude.

So, likewise, it will occasion no inconvenience, if we consider holiness of life as the way, not which procures our admission into the glory of the heavenly kingdom, but through which the elect are conducted by their God to the manifestation of it; since it is his good pleasure to glorify them whom he has sanctified. Only let us not imagine a reciprocal relation of merit and reward which is the error into which the sophists fell, for want of considering the end which we have stated. But how preposterous is it, when the Lord calls our attention to one end, for us to direct our views to another! Nothing is clearer than that the promise of a reward to good works is designed to afford some consolation to the weakness of our flesh, but not to inflate our minds with vain-glory. Whoever, therefore, infers from this, that there is any merit in works, or balances the work against the reward, errs very widely from the true design of God.

V. Pertaining to God's Crowning People for their Works

Therefore, when the Scripture says, that "the Lord, the righteous Judge, shall give" to his people "a crown of righteousness" (2 Tim. 4:8), I not only reply with Augustine— "To whom could the righteous Judge have given a crown, if the Father of mercies had never given grace? and how would it have been an act of righteousness, if not preceded by that grace which justifies the ungodly? how could these due rewards be rendered, unless those unmerited blessings were previously bestowed?"[1] but I further inquire—How could he impute righteousness to our works unless his indulgent mercy had concealed their unrighteousness? How could he esteem them worthy of a reward, unless his infinite goodness had abolished all their demerit of punishment?

Augustine is in the habit of designating eternal life by the word *grace*, because, when it is given as the reward of works, it is conferred on the gratuitous gifts of God. But the Scripture humbles us more, and at the same times exalts us. For besides prohibiting us to glory in works, because they are the gratuitous gifts of God, it likewise teaches us that they are always defiled by some pollutions; so that they cannot satisfy God, if examined according to the rule of his judgment; but it is also added, to prevent our despondency, that they please him merely through his mercy.

Now, though Augustine expresses himself somewhat differently from us, yet that there is no real difference of sentiment will appear from his language to Boniface. After a comparison between two men, the one of a life holy and perfect even to a miracle, the other a man of probity and integrity, yet not so perfect but that many defects might be discovered, he at length makes this inference:

> The latter, whose character appears inferior to the former, on account of the true faith in God by which he lives, and according to which he accuses himself in all his delinquencies, and in all his good works praises God, ascribing the glory to him, the ignominy to himself, and deriving from him both the pardon of his sins and the

---

[1] Augustine, *Grace and Free Will*, et. lib. art.

> love of virtue; this man, I say, when delivered from this life, removes into the presence of Christ. Wherefore, but on account of faith? which, though no man be saved by it without works, (for it is not a reprobate faith, but such as works by love,) yet produces remission of sins, for the just lives by faith [Heb. 10:28]; but without it, works apparently good are perverted into sins.[2]

Here he avows, without any obscurity, that for which we so strenuously contend—that the righteousness of good works depends on their acceptance by the Divine mercy.

VI. Showing How We May Lay Up Treasure in Heaven

Very similar to the foregoing passages is the import of the following: "Make to yourselves friends of the mammon of unrighteousness; that, when you fail, they may receive you into everlasting habitations" (Luke 16:9). "Charge them that are rich in this world, that they be not high-minded, nor trust in uncertain riches, but in the living God; that they do good, that they be rich in good works; laying up in store for themselves a good foundation against the time to come, that they may lay hold on eternal life" (1 Tim. 6:17-19). Here good works are compared to riches, which we may enjoy in the happiness of eternal life. I reply, that we shall never arrive at the true meaning of these passages, unless we advert to the design of the Spirit in such language. If Christ's declaration be true, that "where our treasure is, there will our heart be also" (Matt. 6:21),—as the children of this world are generally intent on the acquisition of those things which conduce to the comfort of the present life, so it ought to be the concern of believers, after they

---

[2] Augustine, *Against Two Pelagian Letters to Pope Boniface*, vol. 3, c. 5.

have been taught that this life will ere long vanish like a dream, to transmit those things which they really wish to enjoy, to that place where they shall possess a perfect and permanent life.

It behooves us, therefore, to imitate the conduct of those who determine to migrate to any new situation, where they have chosen to reside during the remainder of their lives; they send their property before them, without regarding the inconvenience of a temporary absence from it; esteeming their happiness the greater in proportion to the wealth which they possess in the place which they intend for their permanent residence. If we believe heaven to be our country, it is better for us to transmit our wealth thither, than to retain it here, where we may lose it by a sudden removal. But how shall we transmit it? Why, if we communicate to the necessities of the poor; whatever is bestowed on them, the Lord considers as given to himself (Matt. 25:40). Whence that celebrated promise, "He that has pity upon the poor, lends unto the Lord" (Prov. 19:17). Again: "He which sows bountifully shall reap also bountifully" (2 Cor. 9:6). For all things that are bestowed on our brethren in a way of charity, are so many deposits in the hand of the Lord; which he, as a faithful depositary, will one day restore with ample interest.

Are our acts of duty, then, it will be asked, so valuable in the sight of God, that they are like riches reserved in his hand for us? And who can be afraid to assert this, when the Scripture so frequently and plainly declares it? But if any one, from the mere goodness of God, would infer the merit of works, these testimonies will afford no countenance to such an error. For we can infer nothing from them except the indulgence which God in his mercy is disposed to show us, since, in order to animate us to rectitude of conduct, though the duties we perform are unworthy of the least notice from him, yet he suffers not one of them to go unrewarded.

VII. On Righteousness in Enduring Tribulation

But they insist more on the words of the apostle who, to console the Thessalonians under their tribulations, tells them that the design of their infliction is, "that they may be counted worthy of the kingdom of God, for which they also suffer. Seeing," says he, "it is a righteous thing with God to recompense tribulation to them that trouble you; and to you who are troubled, rest with us, when the Lord Jesus shall be revealed from heaven" (2 Thes. 1:5-7). And the author of the Epistle to the Hebrews says, "God is not unrighteous to forget your work and labor of love, which you have showed toward his name, in that you have ministered to the saints" (Heb. 6:10).

To the first passage, I reply, that it indicates no worthiness of merit; but since it is the will of God the Father, that those whom he has chosen as his children be conformed to Christ his first begotten Son (Rom. 8:21); as it was necessary for him first to suffer and then to enter into the glory destined for him (Luke 24:26); so "we must through much tribulation enter into the kingdom of God" (Acts 14:22). The tribulations, therefore, which we suffer for the name of Christ are, as it were, certain marks impressed on us by which God usually distinguishes the sheep of his flock. For this reason, then, we are accounted worthy of the kingdom of God, because we bear in our body the marks of our Lord and Master (Gal. 6:17), which are the badges of the children of God.

The same sentiment is conveyed in the following passages: "Bearing about in the body the dying of the Lord Jesus, that the life also of Jesus might be made manifest in our body" (2 Cor.

4:10). "Being made conformable unto his death, if by any means I might attain unto the resurrection of the dead" (Phil. 3:10-11). The reason which the apostle subjoins tends not to establish any merit, but to confirm the hope of the kingdom of God; as though he had said, 'As it is consistent with the judgment of God to avenge on your enemies those vexations with which they have harassed you, so it is also to grant you respite and repose from those vexations.'

Of the other passage, which represents it as becoming the righteousness of God not to forget our services, so as almost to imply that he would be unrighteous if he did forget them, the meaning is, that in order to arouse our indolence, God has assured us that the labor which we undergo for the glory of his name shall not be in vain. And we should always remember that this promise, as well as all others, would be fraught with no benefit to us, unless it were preceded by the gratuitous covenant of mercy, on which the whole certainty of our salvation must depend. But relying on that covenant, we may securely confide that our services, however unworthy, will not go without a reward from the goodness of God. To confirm us in that expectation, the apostle asserts that God is not unrighteous, but will perform the promise he has once made. This righteousness, therefore, refers rather to the truth of the Divine promise than to the equity of rendering to us anything that is our due. To this purpose there is a remarkable observation of Augustine; and as that holy man has not hesitated frequently to repeat it as deserving of remembrance, so I deem it not unworthy of a constant place in our minds. "The Lord," says he, "is faithful,

Justification by Faith

who has made himself our debtor, not by receiving anything from us, but by promising all things to us."[3]

VIII. Regarding Justification by Virtue

Our Pharisees adduce the following passages of Paul: "Though I have all faith, so that I could remove mountains, and have not charity,[4] I am nothing." Again: "Now abides faith, hope, charity, these three; but the greatest of these is charity" (1 Cor. 13:2, 13). Again: "Above all these things, put on charity, which is the bond of perfectness" (Col. 3:14).

From the first two passages they contend that we are justified rather by charity than by faith; that is, by the superior virtue, as they express it. But this argument is easily overturned. For we have already shown that what is mentioned in the first passage has no reference to true faith. The second we explain to signify true faith, than which he calls charity greater, not as being more meritorious, but because it is more fruitful, more extensive, more generally serviceable, and perpetual in its duration; whereas the use of faith is only temporary. In respect of excellence, the preeminence must be given to the love of God, which is not in this place the subject of Paul's discourse. For the only point which he urges is that, with reciprocal charity, we mutually edify one another in the Lord.

But let us suppose that charity excels faith in all respects, yet what person possessed of sound judgment, or even of the common exercise of reason, would argue from this that it has a greater concern in justification? The power of justifying, attached to faith, consists not in the worthiness of the act. Our justification depends solely on the mercy of God and the merit

---

[3] Augustine, *Exposition of the Psalms*, 32, 109, etc.
[4] Love.

of Christ, which when faith apprehends, it is said to justify us. Now, if we ask our adversaries in what sense they attribute justification to charity, they will reply, that because it is a duty pleasing to God, the merit of it, being accepted by the Divine goodness, is imputed to us for righteousness.

Here we see how curiously their argument proceeds. We assert that faith justifies, not by procuring us a righteousness through its own merit, but as the instrument by which we freely obtain the righteousness of Christ. These men, passing over in silence the mercy of God and making no mention of Christ, in whom is the substance of righteousness, contend that we are justified by the virtue of charity, because it is more excellent than faith; just as though any one should insist that a king in consequence of his superior rank, is more expert at making a shoe than a shoemaker. This one argument affords an ample proof that all the Sorbonic schools are destitute of the least experience of justification by faith. But if any wrangler should yet inquire, why we understand Paul to use the word faith in different acceptations in the same discourse, I am prepared with a substantial reason for such an interpretation. For since those gifts which Paul enumerates are in some respect connected with faith and hope, because they relate to the knowledge of God, he summarily comprises them all under those two words; as though he had said, 'The end of prophecy, and of tongues, of knowledge, and of the gift of interpretation, is to conduct us to the knowledge of God. But we know God in this life only by hope and faith. Therefore, when I mention faith and hope, I comprehend all these things under them.' "And now abides faith, hope, charity, these three;" that is, all gifts, whatever may be their variety, are referred to these. "But the greatest of these is charity."

From the third passage they infer that if "charity is the bond of perfectness," it is therefore the bond of righteousness, which is no other than perfection. Now, to refrain from observing that what Paul calls perfectness is the mutual connection which subsists between the members of a well-constituted church, and to admit that charity constitutes our perfection before God; yet what new advantage will they gain? On the contrary, I shall always object, that we never arrive at that perfection, unless we fulfil all the branches of charity; and hence I shall infer, that since all men are at an immense distance from complete charity, they are destitute of all hope of perfection.

IX. On Keeping the Lord's Commandments
I have no inclination to notice all the passages of Scripture, which the folly of the modern Sorbonists seizes as they occur, and without any reason employs against us. For some of them are so truly ridiculous that I could not even mention them unless I wished to be accounted a fool. I shall therefore conclude this subject after having explained a sentence uttered by Christ, with which they are wonderfully pleased.

To a lawyer, who asked him what was necessary to salvation, he replied, "If you will enter into life, keep the commandments" (Matt. 19:17). What can we wish more, say they, when the Author of grace himself commands to obtain the kingdom of heaven by an observance of the commandments? As though it were not evident that Christ adapted his replies to those with whom he conversed. Here a doctor of the law inquires the method of obtaining happiness, and that not simply, but what men must do in order to attain it. Both the character of the speaker and the inquiry itself induced the Lord to make this

Promise of a Reward

reply. The inquirer, persuaded of the righteousness of the law, possessed a blind confidence in his works. Besides, he only inquired what were those works of righteousness by which salvation might be procured. He is therefore justly referred to the law, which contains a perfect mirror of righteousness. We also explicitly declare, that if life be sought by works, it is indispensably requisite to keep the commandments. And this doctrine is necessary to be known by Christians; for how should they flee for refuge to Christ, if they did not acknowledge themselves to have fallen from the way of life upon the precipice of death? And how could they know how far they have wandered from the way of life, without a previous knowledge of what that way of life is? It is then, therefore, that Christ is presented to them as the asylum of salvation, when they perceive the vast difference between their own lives and the Divine righteousness, which consists in the observance of the law.

The sum of the whole is that if we seek salvation by works, we must keep the commandments, by which we are taught perfect righteousness. But to stop here, would be failing in the midst of our course, for to keep the commandments is a task to which none of us are equal. Being excluded, then, from the righteousness of the law, we are under the necessity of resorting to some other refuge, namely, to faith in Christ. Wherefore, as the Lord, knowing this doctor of the law to be inflated with a vain confidence in his works, recalls his attention to the law, that it may teach him his own character as a sinner, obnoxious to the tremendous sentence of eternal death, so, in another place, addressing those who have already been humbled under this knowledge, he omits all mention of the law, and consoles them with a promise of grace—"Come unto me, all you that labor and are heavy laden, and I will give you rest; and you shall find rest unto your souls" (Matt. 11:28-29).

X. Is Faith a Work?

At length, after our adversaries have wearied themselves with perversions of Scripture, they betake themselves to subtleties and sophisms. They cavil that faith is in some places called a work (John 6:29), and hence they infer that we improperly oppose faith to works. As though faith procured righteousness for us by its intrinsic merit, as an act of obedience to the Divine will, and not rather because by embracing the Divine mercy, it seals to our hearts the righteousness of Christ, which that mercy offers to us in the preaching of the gospel. The reader will pardon me for not dwelling on the confutation of such follies; for they require nothing to refute them but their own weakness. But I wish briefly to answer one objection, which has some appearance of reason, to prevent its being the source of any difficulty to persons who have had but little experience.

Since common sense dictates that opposites are subject to similar rules, and as all sins are imputed to us for unrighteousness, they maintain it to be reasonable, on the other hand, that all good works should be imputed to us for righteousness. Those who reply that the condemnation of men proceeds from unbelief alone, and not from particular sins, do not satisfy me. I agree with them that incredulity is the fountain and root of all evils. For it is the original defection from God, which is afterwards followed by particular transgressions of the law. But as they appear to fix one and the same rule for good and evil works in forming a judgment of righteousness or unrighteousness, here I am obliged to dissent from them. For the righteousness of works is the perfect obedience of the law.

We cannot therefore be righteous by works, unless we follow this straight line throughout the whole of our lives. The first deviation from it is a lapse into unrighteousness. Hence it appears that righteousness arises not from one or a few works, but from an inflexible and indefatigable observance of the Divine will. But the rule of judging of unrighteousness is very different. For he who has committed fornication or theft is for one transgression liable to the sentence of death, because he has offended against the divine Majesty. These disputants of ours, therefore, fall into an error for want of adverting to the decision of James, that "whosoever shall keep the whole law, and yet offend in one point, he is guilty of all." For he that said, "Do not commit adultery," said also, "Do not kill," &c. (Jas. 2:10-11). It ought not, therefore, to be deemed absurd, when we say that death is the reward justly due to every sin, because they are all and every one deserving of the indignation and vengeance of God. But it will be a weak argument to infer, on the contrary, that one good work will reconcile a man to God, whose wrath he has incurred by a multitude of sins.

9

ON CHRISTIAN LIBERTY

I. Christian Liberty as an Appendix to Justification
We have now to treat of Christian liberty, an explanation of which ought not to be omitted in a treatise which is designed to comprehend a compendious summary of evangelical doctrine. For it is a subject of the first importance, and unless it be well understood, our consciences scarcely venture to undertake anything without doubting, experience in many things hesitation and reluctance, and are always subject to fluctuations and fears. But especially it is an appendix to justification, and affords no small assistance towards the knowledge of its influence. Hence they who sincerely fear God will experience the incomparable advantage of that doctrine, which impious scoffers pursue with their railleries; because in the spiritual intoxication with which they are seized, they allow themselves the most unbounded impudence.

Wherefore this is the proper time to introduce the subject; and though we have slightly touched upon it on some former occasions, yet it was useful to defer the full discussion of it to this place; because as soon as any mention is made of Christian liberty, then either inordinate passions rage, or violent emotions arise, unless timely opposition be made to those wanton spirits, who most nefariously corrupt things which are otherwise the best. For some, under the pretext of this liberty, cast off all obedience to God, and precipitate themselves into the most unbridled licentiousness; and some despise it, supposing it to be subversive of all moderation, order, and moral distinctions. What can we do in this case, surrounded by such difficulties? Shall we entirely discard Christian liberty, and so preclude the occasion of such dangers? But, as we have observed, unless this be understood, there can be no right knowledge of Christ, or of evangelical truth, or of internal peace of mind. We should rather exert ourselves to prevent the suppression of such a necessary branch of doctrine, and at the same time to obviate those absurd objections which are frequently deduced from it.

II. Part One: Forsaking All Righteousness of Law

Christian liberty, according to my judgment, consists of three parts. The first part is that the consciences of believers, when seeking an assurance of their justification before God, should raise themselves above the law, and forget all the righteousness of the law. For since the law, as we have elsewhere demonstrated, leaves no man righteous, either we must be excluded from all hope of justification, or it is necessary for us to be delivered from it, and that so completely as not to have any dependence on works. For he who imagines that, in order to obtain righteousness, he must produce any works, however small, can fix no limit or boundary, but renders himself a debtor to the whole law. Avoiding, therefore, all mention of the law, and dismissing all thought of our own works, in reference to justification, we must embrace the Divine mercy alone, and turning our eyes from ourselves, fix them solely on Christ.

For the question is not how we can be righteous, but how, though unrighteous and unworthy, we can be considered as righteous. And the conscience that desires to attain any certainty respecting this must give no admission to the law. Nor will this authorize any one to conclude that the law is of no use to believers, whom it still continues to instruct and exhort, and stimulate to duty, although it has no place in their consciences before the tribunal of God. For these two things, being very different, require to be properly and carefully distinguished by us. The whole life of Christians ought to be an exercise of piety, since they are called to sanctification (Eph. 1:4; 1 Thes. 4:3, 7). It is the office of the law to remind them of their duty, and thereby to excite them to the pursuit of holiness and integrity. But when their consciences are solicitous how God may be propitiated, what answer they shall make, and on what they shall rest their confidence, if called to his tribunal, there must then be no consideration of the requisitions of the law, but Christ alone must be proposed for righteousness, who exceeds all the perfection of the law.

III. The Testimony of Galatians

On this point turns almost the whole argument of the Epistle to the Galatians. For that they are erroneous expositors who maintain that Paul there contends only for liberty from ceremonies, may be proved from the topics of his reasoning. Such as these: "Christ has redeemed us from the curse of the law, being made a curse for us" (Gal. 3:13). Again:

JUSTIFICATION BY FAITH

> Stand fast, therefore, in the liberty wherewith Christ has made us free, and be not entangled again with the yoke of bondage. Behold, I Paul say unto you, that if you be circumcised, Christ shall profit you nothing. Every man that is circumcised is a debtor to do the whole law. Christ is become of no effect unto you, whosoever of you are justified by the law; you are fallen from grace (Gal. 5:1-4).

These passages certainly comprehend something more exalted than a freedom from ceremonies. I confess, indeed, that Paul is there treating of ceremonies, because he is contending with the false apostles who attempted to introduce again into the Christian Church the ancient shadows of the law, which had been abolished by the advent of Christ. But for the decision of this question it was necessary to discuss some higher topics in which the whole controversy lay.

First, because the brightness of the gospel was obscured by those Jewish shadows, he shows that in Christ we have a complete exhibition of all those things which were adumbrated by the ceremonies of Moses. Secondly, because these impostors instilled into the people the very pernicious opinion, that this ceremonial obedience was sufficient to merit the Divine favor, he principally contends that believers ought not to suppose that they can obtain righteousness before God by any works of the law, much less by those inferior elements. And he at the same time teaches that from the condemnation of the law, which otherwise impends over all men, they are delivered by the cross of Christ, that they may rely with perfect security on him alone—a topic which properly belongs to our present subject. Lastly, he asserts the liberty of the consciences of believers, which ought to be laid under no obligation in things that are not necessary.

IV. Part Two: The Conscience's Obedience to God's Will

The second part of Christian liberty, which is dependent on the first, is that their consciences do not observe the law, as being under any legal obligation; but that, being liberated from the yoke of the law, they yield a voluntary obedience to the will of God. For being possessed with perpetual terrors, as long as they remain under the dominion of the law, they will never engage with alacrity and promptitude in the service of God, unless they have previously received this liberty. We shall more easily and clearly discover the design of these things from an example.

The precept of the law is, "You shall love the Lord thy God with all your heart, and with all your soul, and with all your might" (Deut. 6:5). That this command may be fulfilled, our soul must be previously divested of every other perception and thought, our heart must be freed from all desires, and our might must be collected and contracted to this one point. Those who, compared with others, have made a very considerable progress in the way of the Lord, are yet at an immense distance from this perfection. For though they love God with their soul, and with sincere affection of heart, yet they have still much of their heart and soul occupied by carnal desires, which retard their progress towards God. They do indeed press forward with strong exertions, but the flesh partly debilitates their strength, and partly attracts it to itself. What can they do in this case, when they perceive that they are so far from observing the law? They wish, they aspire, they endeavor, but they do nothing with the perfection that is required. If they advert to the law, they see that every work they attempt or meditate is accursed. Nor is there the least reason for any person to deceive himself, by concluding that an action is not necessarily altogether evil, because it is imperfect, and that therefore the good part of it is accepted by God. For the law, requiring perfect love, condemns all imperfection, unless its rigor be mitigated. Let him consider his work, therefore, which he wished to be thought partly good, and he will find that very work to be a transgression of the law, because it is imperfect.

V. The Joy of the Liberated Soul!
See how all our works, if estimated according to the rigor of the law, are subject to its curse. How, then, could unhappy souls apply themselves with alacrity to any work for which they could expect to receive nothing but a curse? On the contrary, if they are liberated from the severe exaction of the law, or rather from the whole of its rigor, and hear God calling them with paternal gentleness, then with cheerfulness and prompt alacrity they will answer to his call and follow his guidance. In short, they who are bound by the yoke of the law are like slaves who have certain daily tasks appointed by their masters. They think they have done nothing, and presume not to enter into the presence of their masters without having finished the work prescribed to them.

But children, who are treated by their parents in a more liberal manner, hesitate not to present to them their imperfect, and in some respects faulty works, in confidence that their obedience and promptitude of mind will be accepted by them, though they have not performed all that they wished. Such children ought we to be, feeling a certain confidence that our services, however small, rude, and imperfect, will be approved by our most indulgent Father. This he also confirms to us by the prophet: "I will spare them," says he, "as a man spares his own son that serves him" (Mal. 3:17); where it is evident, from the mention of *service*, that the word *spare* is used to denote indulgence, or an overlooking of faults. And we have great need of this confidence, without which all our endeavors will be vain; for God considers us as serving him in none of our works, but such as are truly done by us to his honor. But how can this be done amidst those terrors, where it is a matter of doubt whether our works offend God or honor him?

VI. The Testimony of Hebrews

This is the reason why the author of the Epistle to the Hebrews refers to faith, and estimates only by faith, all the good works which are recorded of the holy patriarchs (Heb. 11:2). On this liberty there is a remarkable passage in the Epistle to the Romans where Paul reasons that sin ought not to have dominion over us, because we are not under the law, but under grace (Rom. 6:14). For after he had exhorted believers, "Let not sin, therefore, reign in your mortal body; neither yield your members as instruments of unrighteousness; but yield yourselves unto God, as those that are alive from the dead, and your members as instruments of righteousness unto God" (Rom. 6:12-13)—they might, on the contrary, object that they yet carried about with them the flesh full of inordinate desires, and that sin dwelt in them; but he adds the consolation furnished by their liberty from the law; as though he had said, 'Although you do not yet experience sin to be destroyed, and righteousness living in you in perfection, yet you have no cause for terror and dejection of mind, as if God were perpetually offended on account of your remaining sin; because by grace you are emancipated from the law, that your works may not be judged according to that rule.' But those who infer that we may commit sin because we are not under the law, may be assured that they have no concern with this liberty, the end of which is to animate us to virtue.

VII. Part Three: No Obligation to External Things
The third part of Christian liberty teaches us that we are bound by no obligation before God respecting external things, which in themselves are indifferent; but that we may indifferently sometimes use, and at other times omit them. And the knowledge of this liberty also is very necessary for us; for without it we shall have no tranquility of conscience, nor will there be any end of superstitions.

Many in the present age think it a folly to raise any dispute concerning the free use of meats, of days, and of habits, and similar subjects, considering these things as frivolous and nugatory; but they are of greater importance than is generally believed. For when the conscience has once fallen into the snare, it enters a long and inextricable labyrinth from which it is afterwards difficult to escape; if a man begin to doubt the lawfulness of using flax in sheets, shirts, handkerchiefs, napkins, and table cloths, neither will he be certain respecting hemp, and at last he will doubt of the lawfulness of using tow; for he will consider with himself whether he cannot eat without table cloths or napkins, whether he cannot do without handkerchiefs. If anyone imagine delicate food to be unlawful, he will ere long have no tranquility before God in eating brown bread and common viands, while he remembers that he might support his body with meat of a quality still inferior. If he hesitate respecting good wine, he will afterwards be unable with any peace of conscience to drink the most vapid; and at last he will not presume even to touch purer and sweeter water than others.

In short, he will come to think it criminal to step over a twig that lies across his path. For this is the commencement of no rival controversy; but the dispute is whether the use of certain things be agreeable to God whose will ought to guide all our resolutions and all our actions. The necessary consequence is that some are hurried by despair into a vortex of confusion from which they see no way of escape; and some, despising God, and casting off all fear of him, make a way of ruin for themselves. For all who are involved in such doubts, which way so ever they turn their views, behold something offensive to their consciences presenting itself on every side.

VIII. The Testimony of Romans

"I know," says Paul, "that there is nothing unclean of itself; but to him that esteems anything to be unclean, to him it is unclean" (Rom. 14:14). In these words he makes all external things subject to our liberty, provided that our minds have regard to this liberty before God. But if any superstitious notion cause us to scruple, those things which were naturally pure become contaminated to us. Wherefore he subjoins, "Happy is he that condemns not himself in that which he allows. And he that doubts is condemned if he eat, because he eats not of faith; for whatsoever is not of faith is sin" (Rom. 14:22-23). Are not they who, in these perplexities show their superior boldness by the security of their presumption, guilty of departing from God? whilst they who are deeply affected with the true fear of God, when they are even constrained to admit many things to which their own consciences are averse, are filled with terror and consternation. No persons of this description receive any of the

JUSTIFICATION BY FAITH

gifts of God with thanksgiving, by which alone Paul, nevertheless, declares them to be all sanctified to our use (1 Tim. 4:5). I mean a thanksgiving proceeding from a mind which acknowledges the beneficence and goodness of God in the blessings he bestows. For many of them, indeed, apprehend the good things which they use to be from God, whom they praise in his works; but not being persuaded that they are given to them, how could they give thanks to God as the giver of them?

We see, in short, the tendency of this liberty, which is, that without any scruple of conscience or perturbation of mind, we should devote the gifts of God to that use for which he has given them; by which confidence our souls may have peace with him, and acknowledge his liberality towards us. For this comprehends all ceremonies, the observation of which is left free, that the conscience may not be bound by any obligation to observe them, but may remember that by the goodness of God it may use them, or abstain from them, as shall be most conducive to edification.

IX. The Nature and Efficacy of Christian Liberty

Now, it must be carefully observed that Christian liberty is in all its branches a spiritual thing. All the virtue of which consists in appeasing terrified consciences before God, whether they are disquieted and solicitous concerning the remission of their sins, or are anxious to know if their works, which are imperfect and contaminated by the defilements of the flesh, be acceptable to God; or are tormented concerning the use of things that are indifferent. Wherefore they are guilty of perverting its meaning, who either make it the pretext of their irregular appetites, that they may abuse the Divine blessings to the purposes of sensuality, or who suppose that there is no liberty but what is used before men, and therefore in the exercise of it totally disregard their weak brethren. The former of these sins is the more common in the present age.

There is scarcely any one, whom his wealth permits to be sumptuous, who is not delighted with luxurious splendor in his entertainments, in his dress, and in his buildings; who does not desire a preeminence in every species of luxury; who does not strangely flatter himself on his elegance. And all these things are defended under the pretext of Christian liberty. They allege that they are things indifferent; this I admit, provided they be indifferently used. But where they are too ardently coveted, proudly boasted, or luxuriously lavished, these things, of themselves otherwise indifferent, are completely polluted by such vices. This passage of Paul makes an excellent distinction respecting things which are indifferent: "Unto the pure all things are pure; but unto them that are defiled and unbelieving is nothing pure; but even their mind and conscience is defiled" (Titus 1:15). For why are curses denounced on rich men who "receive their consolation," who are "satiated," who "now laugh," who "lie on beds of ivory," who "join field to field," who "have the harp, and the lyre, and the tabret, and wine in their feasts" (Luke 6:24-25; Amos 6:1ff.; Isa. 5:8ff.)? Ivory and gold, and riches of all kinds, are certainly blessings of Divine Providence, not only permitted, but expressly designed for the use of men; nor are we anywhere prohibited to laugh, or to be satiated with food, or to annex new possessions to those already enjoyed by ourselves or by our ancestors, or to be delighted with musical harmony, or to drink wine. This indeed is true; but amidst an abundance of all things, to be immersed in sensual delights, to inebriate the heart and mind with present pleasures, and perpetually to grasp at new ones,—these things are very remote from a legitimate use of the Divine blessings.

Let them banish, therefore, immoderate cupidity, excessive profusion, vanity, and arrogance; that with a pure conscience they may make a proper use of the gifts of God. When their hearts shall be formed to this sobriety, they will have a rule for the legitimate enjoyment of them. On the contrary, without this moderation, even common and ordinary pleasures are charge able with excess. For it is truly observed that a proud heart frequently dwells under coarse and ragged garments, and that simplicity and humility are sometimes concealed under purple and fine linen. Let all men, in their respective stations, whether of poverty, of competence, or of splendor, live in the remembrance of this truth, that God confers his blessings on them for the support of life, not for luxury; and let them consider this as the law of Christian liberty, that they learn the lesson which Paul had learned, when he said, "I have learned, in whatsoever state I am, therewith to be content. I know both how to be abased, and I know how to abound: everywhere and in all things I am instructed, both to be full and to be hungry, both to abound and to suffer need" (Phil. 4:11-12).

X. Christian Liberty and Weak Brethren

Many persons err likewise in this respect that, as if their liberty would not be perfectly secure unless witnessed by men, they make an indiscriminate and imprudent use of it—a disorderly practice, which occasions frequent offense to their weak brethren. There are some to be found, in the present day, who imagine their liberty would be abridged, if they were not to enter on the enjoyment of it by eating animal food on Friday. Their eating is not the subject of my reprehension; but their minds require to be divested of this false notion. For they ought to consider that they obtain no advantage from their liberty before men, but with God; and that it consists in abstinence as well as in use. If they apprehend it to be immaterial in God's view, whether they eat animal food or eggs, whether their garments be scarlet or black, it is quite sufficient. The conscience, to which the benefit of this liberty was due, is now emancipated. Therefore, though they abstain from flesh, and wear but one color, during all the rest of their lives, this is no diminution of their freedom. Nay, because they are free, they therefore abstain with a free conscience. But they fall into a very pernicious error in disregarding the infirmity of their brethren, which it becomes us to bear, so as not rashly to do anything which would give them the least offense. But it will be said that it is sometimes right to assert our liberty before men. This I confess; yet the greatest caution and moderation must be observed, lest we cast off all concern for the weak, whom God has so strongly recommended to our regards.

XI. Examining Offenses Pertaining to Christian Liberty

I shall now, therefore, make some observations concerning offenses; how they are to be discriminated, what are to be avoided, and what are to be disregarded; whence we may afterwards determine what room there is for our liberty in our intercourse with mankind. I approve of the common distinction between an offense given and an offense taken, since it is plainly countenanced by Scripture, and is likewise sufficiently significant of the thing intended to be expressed.

If you do anything at a wrong time or place, or with an unseasonable levity, or wantonness, or temerity, by which the weak and inexperienced are offended, it must be termed an offense given by you; because it arises from your fault. And an offense is always said to be given in any action, the fault of which proceeds from the performer of that action. An offense taken is when any transaction, not otherwise unseasonable or culpable is, through malevolence, or some perverse disposition, construed into an occasion of offense. For in this instance the offense is not given, but taken without reason by such perverseness of construction. The first species of offense affects none but the weak; the second is created by moroseness of temper, and Pharisaical superciliousness. Wherefore we shall denominate the former, the offense of the weak, the latter, that of Pharisees; and we shall so temper the use of our liberty, that it ought to submit to the ignorance of weak brethren, but not at all to the austerity of Pharisees.

For our duty to the weak, Paul fully shows in many places. "Him that is weak in the faith receive you." Again: "Let us not therefore judge one another anymore; but judge this rather, that no man put a stumbling-block or an occasion to fall in his brother's way" (Rom. 14:1, 13); and much more to the same import, which were better examined in its proper connection than recited here. The sum of all is that "we, then, that are strong, ought to bear the infirmities of the weak, and not to please ourselves. Let every one of us please his neighbor for his good to edification" (Rom. 15:1-2). In another place: "But take heed lest by any means this liberty of yours become a stumbling-block to them that are weak" (1 Cor. 8:9). Again: "Whatsoever is sold in the shambles, that eat; asking no questions for conscience' sake; conscience, I say, not thine own, but of the other." In short, "Give none offense, neither to the Jews, nor to the Gentiles, nor to the Church of God" (1 Cor. 10:25, 29, 32). In another place also: "Brethren, you have been called unto liberty; only use not liberty for an occasion to the flesh, but by love serve one another" (Gal. 5:13). The meaning of this is that our liberty is not given us to be used in opposition to our weak neighbors, to whom charity obliges us to do every possible service; but rather in order that, having peace with God in our minds, we may also live peaceably among men. But how much attention should be paid to an offense taken by Pharisees, we learn from our Lord's injunction, "Let them alone; they be blind leaders of the blind" (Matt. 25:14). The disciples had informed him that the Pharisees were offended with his discourse. He replies that they are to be let alone, and their offense disregarded.

XII. The Weak and the Pharisees

But the subject is still pending in uncertainty, unless we know whom we are to account weak, and whom we are to consider as Pharisees; without which distinction, I see no use of liberty in the midst of offenses, but such as must be attended with the greatest danger. But Paul appears to me to have very clearly decided, both by doctrine and examples, how far our liberty should be either moderated or asserted on the occurrence of offenses.

When he made Timothy his associate, he circumcised him (Acts 16:3); but could not be induced to circumcise Titus (Gal. 2:3). Here was a difference in his proceedings, but no change of mind or of purpose. In the circumcision of Timothy, "though he was free from all men, yet he made himself servant unto all;" and says he, "Unto the Jews I became as a Jew, that I might gain the Jews; to them that are under the law, as under the law, that I might gain them that are under the law: I am made all things to all men, that I might by all means save some" (1 Cor. 9:19, 20,

22). Thus we have a proper moderation of liberty, if it may be indifferently restricted with any advantage.

His reason for resolutely refraining from circumcising Titus, he declares in the following words: "But neither Titus, who was with me, being a Greek, was compelled to be circumcised, and that because of false brethren unawares brought in, who came in privily to spy out our liberty which we have in Christ Jesus, that they might bring us into bondage; to whom we gave place by subjection, no, not for an hour; that the truth of the gospel might continue with you" (Gal. 2:3-5). We also are under the necessity of vindicating our liberty, if it be endangered in weak consciences by the iniquitous requisitions of false apostles. We must at all times study charity, and keep in view the edification of our neighbor. "All things (says Paul) are lawful for me, but all things are not expedient: all things are lawful for me, but all things edify not. Let no man seek his own, but every man another's" (1 Cor. 10:23-24).

Nothing can be plainer than this rule, that our liberty should be used if it conduces to our neighbor's edification; but that if it be not beneficial to our neighbor, it should be abridged. There are some who pretend to imitate the prudence of Paul in refraining from the exercise of liberty, while they are doing anything but exercising the duties of charity. For to promote their own tranquility, they wish all mention of liberty to be buried; whereas it is no less advantageous to our neighbors sometimes to use our liberty to their benefit and edification, than at other times to moderate it for their accommodation. But a pious man considers this liberty in external things as granted him in order that he may be the better prepared for all the duties of charity.

XIII. The Right Application of Liberty

But whatever I have advanced respecting the avoidance of offenses, I wish to be referred to indifferent and unimportant things. For necessary duties must not be omitted through fear of any offense. As our liberty should be subject to charity, so charity itself ought to be subservient to the purity of faith. It becomes us, indeed, to have regard to charity; but we must not offend God for the love of our neighbor. We cannot approve the intemperance of those who do nothing but in a tumultuous manner, and who prefer violent measures to lenient ones. Nor must we listen to those, who, while they show themselves the leaders in a thousand species of impiety, pretend that they are obliged to act in such a manner, that they may give no offense to their neighbors; as though they are not at the same time fortifying the consciences of their neighbors in sin; especially since they are always sticking in the same mire without any hope of deliverance.

And whether their neighbor is to be instructed by doctrine or by example, they maintain that he ought to be fed with milk, though they are infecting him with the worst and most pernicious notions. Paul tells the Corinthians, "I have fed you with milk" (1 Cor. 3:2); but if the Popish mass had been then introduced among them, would he have united in that pretended sacrifice in order to feed them with milk? Certainly not; for milk is not poison. They are guilty of falsehood, therefore, in saying that they feed those whom they cruelly murder under the appearance of such flatteries. But admitting that such dissimulation is to be approved for a time, how long will they feed their children with the same milk? For if they never grow, so as to be able to bear even some light meat, it is a clear proof that they were never fed with milk.

I am prevented from pushing this controversy with them any further at present, by two reasons—first, because their absurdities scarcely deserve a refutation, being justly despised by all men of sound understanding; secondly, having done this at large in particular treatises, I am unwilling to travel the same ground over again. Only let the readers remember that with whatever offenses Satan and the world may endeavor to divert us from the ordinances of God, or to retard our pursuit of what he enjoins, yet we must nevertheless strenuously advance; and moreover, that whatever dangers threaten us, we are not at liberty to deviate even a hair's breadth from his command, and that it is not lawful under any pretext to attempt anything but what he permits.

XIV. Living with a Clear Conscience

Now, since the consciences of believers, being privileged with the liberty which we have described, have been delivered by the favor of Christ from all necessary obligation to the observance of those things in which the Lord has been pleased they should be left free, we conclude that they are exempt from all human authority. For it is not right that Christ should lose the acknowledgments due to such kindness, or our consciences the benefit of it. Neither is that to be accounted a trivial thing, which we see cost Christ so much; which he estimated not with gold or silver, but with his own blood (1 Pet. 1:18-19); so that Paul hesitates not to assert that his death is rendered vain, if we suffer our souls to be in subjection to men (Gal. 5:1, 4). For his sole object in some chapters of his Epistle to the Galatians is to prove that Christ is obscured, or rather abolished, with respect to us, unless our consciences continue in their liberty; from which they are certainly fallen, if they can be ensnared in the bonds of laws and ordinances at the pleasure of men (1 Cor. 7:23). But as it is a subject highly worthy of being understood, so it needs a more diffuse and perspicuous explanation. For as soon as a word is mentioned concerning the abrogation of human establishments, great tumults are excited, partly by seditious persons, partly by cavillers; as though all obedience of men were at once subverted and destroyed.

XV. Spiritual vs. Political Government

To prevent anyone from falling into this error, let us therefore consider, in the first place, that man is under two kinds of government—one spiritual, by which the conscience is formed to piety and the service of God; the other political, by which a man is instructed in the duties of humanity and civility, which are to be observed in an intercourse with mankind. They are generally, and not improperly, denominated the spiritual and the temporal jurisdiction; indicating that the former species of government pertains to the life of the soul, and that the latter relates to the concerns of the present state; not only to the provision of food and clothing, but to the enactment of laws to regulate a man's life among his neighbors by the rules of holiness, integrity, and sobriety.

For the former has its seat in the interior of the mind, whilst the latter only directs the external conduct: one may be termed a spiritual kingdom, and the other a political one. But these two, as we have distinguished them, always require to be considered separately; and while the one is under discussion, the mind must be abstracted from all consideration of the other. For man contains, as it were, two worlds, capable of being governed by various rulers and various laws. This distinction will prevent what the gospel inculcates concerning spiritual liberty from being misapplied to political regulations; as though Christians were less subject to the external government of human laws, because their consciences have been set at liberty before God; as though their freedom of spirit necessarily exempted them from all carnal servitude. Again, because even in those constitutions which seem to pertain to the spiritual kingdom, there may possibly be some deception, it is necessary to discriminate between these also; which are to be accounted legitimate, as according with the Divine word, and which, on the contrary, ought not to be received among believers. Of civil government I shall treat in another place. Of ecclesiastical laws also I forbear to speak at present; because a full discussion of them will be proper in the Fourth Book, where we shall treat of the power of the Church. But we shall conclude the present argument in the following manner:

The question, which, as I have observed, is in itself not very obscure or intricate, greatly perplexes many, because they do not distinguish with sufficient precision between the external jurisdiction and the court of conscience. The difficulty is increased by Paul's injunction to obey magistrates "not only for wrath, but also for conscience' sake" (Rom. 8:1, 5); from which it should follow that the conscience also is bound by political laws. But if this were true, it would supersede all that we have already said, or are now about to say, respecting spiritual government.

For the solution of this difficulty, it will be of use, first, to know what conscience is. And the definition of it must be derived from the etymology of the word. For as, when men apprehend the knowledge of things in the mind and understanding, they are thence said *scire*, "to know," whence is derived the word *scientia*, "science" or "knowledge;" so when they have a sense of Divine justice, as an additional witness, which permits them not to conceal their sins, or to elude accusation at the tribunal of the supreme Judge, this sense is termed *conscientia*, "conscience." For it is a kind of medium between God and man; because it does not suffer a man to suppress what he knows within himself, but pursues him till it brings him to conviction.

This is what Paul means by "their conscience also bearing witness, and their thoughts accusing, or else excusing, one another" (Rom. 2:15). Simple knowledge might remain, as it were, confined within a man. This sentiment, therefore, which places man before the Divine tribunal, is appointed, as it were, to watch over man, to observe and examine all his secrets, that nothing may remain enveloped in darkness. Hence the old proverb, "Conscience is as a thousand witnesses." For the same reason Peter speaks of "the answer of a good conscience towards God" (1 Pet. 3:21), to express our tranquility of mind, when, persuaded of the favor of Christ, we present ourselves with boldness in the presence of God. And the author of the Epistle to the Hebrews expresses absolution or freedom from every future charge of sin, by "having no more conscience of sin" (Heb. 10:2).

XVI. Pursuing the Christian Life with a Good Conscience

Therefore, as works respect men, so conscience regards God; so that a good conscience is no other than inward integrity of heart. In which sense Paul says that "the end of the commandment is charity, out of a pure heart, and of a good conscience, and of faith unfeigned" (1 Tim. 1:5). Afterwards also, in the same chapter, he shows how widely it differs from understanding, saying that "some, having put away a good conscience, concerning faith have made shipwreck" (1 Tim. 1:19). For these words indicate that it is a lively inclination to the service of God, and a sincere pursuit of piety and holiness of life.

Sometimes, indeed, it is likewise extended to men; as when the same apostle declares, "Herein do I exercise myself, to have always a conscience void of offense toward God and toward men" (Acts 24:16). But the reason of this assertion is that the fruits of a good conscience reach even to men. But in strict propriety of speech it has to do with God alone, as I have already observed. Hence it is that a law which simply binds a man without relation to other men, or any consideration of them is said to bind the conscience. For example, God not only enjoins the preservation of the mind chaste and pure from every libidinous desire, but prohibits all obscenity of language and external lasciviousness.

The observance of this law is incumbent on my conscience, though there were not another man existing in the world. Thus he who transgresses the limits of temperance, not only sins by giving a bad example to his brethren, but contracts guilt on his conscience before God. Things in themselves indifferent are to be guided by other considerations. It is our duty to abstain from them, if they tend to the least offense, yet without violating our liberty of conscience. So Paul speaks concerning meat consecrated to idols: "If any man say unto you, 'This is offered in sacrifice to idols,' eat not for conscience' sake; conscience, I say, not thine own, but of the other" (1 Cor. 10:28–29). A pious man would be guilty of sin who, being previously admonished, should, nevertheless, eat such meat. But though, with respect to his brother, abstinence is necessary for him, as it is enjoined by God, yet he ceases not to retain liberty of conscience. We see, then, how this law, though it binds the external action, leaves the conscience free.

Scripture Index

Genesis
4:4...............................75
6:3...............................66
6:5...............................65
8:21..............................65
12:2-3..........................146
13:16...........................146
15:5.............................146
15:6.............................136
22:16-18......................146

Exodus
33:19............................21

Leviticus
18:5........................81, 120

Deuteronomy
4:6...............................75
6:5..............................167
6:25.............................127
7:9..............................124
7:12-13.........................118
11:26...........................118
24:13............................127
27:26..................43, 81, 130
29:19-20........................124
30:15............................118

1 Samuel
26:23............................140

2 Samuel
22:20-21.........................125

1 Kings
1:21................................4
8:23..............................124

2 Kings
20:3..............................89

Nehemiah
1:5..............................124

Job
4:17-20...........................43
4:18.............................130
9:2, 3............................44
9:20..............................49
10:15.............................85
14:4..............................49
15:15............................130
15:15, 16.........................43
15:16.............................49
25:4, 6...........................49
25:5.............................130
41:11.............................70

Psalms
1:1..............................132
7:8..............................138
14:1-3............................66
15:1-2...........................126
17:1, 3..........................138
18:21, 23, 24....................139
18:27.............................50
19:12............................120
23:4..............................62
25:10-11.........................120
26:1, 4, 9-11....................139
32:1-2...........................132
36:1..............................66
51:5..............................21
63:3.............................140
94:11.............................65
106:3............................132

187

Psalms Continued
106:30–31	127
106:31	129
111:10	75
112:1	132
119:1	132
119:76, 77	60
130:3	42, 140
130:4	114
143:2	44, 85, 140

Proverbs
1:7	75
9:10	75
12:14	143
12:28	141
13:13	143
14:21	132
14:26	89
15:8	75
16:2	49
19:17	153
20:7	141
20:9	58
21:2	49

Ecclesiastes
7:20	76
9:1	61
16:14	100

Song of Solomon
5:3	115

Isaiah
1:12	85
1:13, 16	75
4:2	84, 85
5:8ff	173
9:6	62
33:14, 15	42
33:14–15	126
41:3	86
45:23–25	57
45:25	86
53:6	49
53:11	13
55:1	101
57:15	51
59:1, 2	36
59:15, 16	71
59:17	25
61:1–3	52
66:2	51

Jeremiah
5:3	76
7:5–7	118
9:23–24	56
17:9	65
23:6	13
33:16	13

Ezekiel
18:24	77
20:43–44	56
33:14–15	141
36:32	98

Hosea
2:19, 23	72
14:4	72

Amos
6:1ff	173

Zephaniah
3:11, 12	51

Haggai
2:11–14	74

Zechariah
3:9, 10 62

Malachi
3:17 169
4:2 23

Matthew
5:3, 5, 7 132
5:12 143
5:16 113
6:21 152
9:13 .... 52, 71
11:28 52
11:28–29 160
11:29 113
16:27 .... 114, 143
19:17 158
20:1ff 147
23:12 51
25:14 177
25:21, 29 101
25:34 .... 145, 148
25:34–36 143
25:40 153
28:18 103

Mark
10:30 148

Luke
1:6 128
1:74–75 111
1:77 37
6:23 143
6:24–25 173
7:29, 35 3
9:23 106
14:11 51
16:9 152

16:15 .... 4, 44
17:10 .... 83, 98
18:13 51
18:14 .... 5, 51
24:26 154

John
1:12 102
3:16 87
5:24 104
5:25 69
5:29 143
6:27 144
6:29 160
8:12 23
10:28, 29 102
12:43 15
13:15 113
17:19 24

Acts
9:15 45
10:34–35 122
13:38, 39 38
13:38–39 5
13:39 103
14:22 154
15:9 76
16:3 177
20:28 13
24:16 184

Romans
1:17 33
2:6 .... 114, 143
2:9–10 143
2:13 .... 28, 137
2:15 183
3:10–18 xix
3:10ff 31

Romans Continued
3:11......................................66
3:19..............................55, 57
3:20......................................34
3:21......................................32
3:21, 24, 28.......................33
3:23ff...................................87
3:24...............................6, 104
3:24–25...............................25
3:26........................4, 55, 57
3:27......................................26
3:28....................................xvii
4:2................................26, 33
4:2–3...................................32
4:3......................................129
4:3–24.................................xx
4:4..26
4:4, 5...................................35
4:5..................................4, 10
4:6..35
4:6–8.......................6, 19, 37
4:7..79
4:7–8.................................132
4:9..79
4:14......................................59
4:15......................................34
4:16................................32, 60
4:17......................................70
5:1..62
5:5..62
5:6, 10.................................72
5:8–10.................................36
5:12–21................................xx
5:19...............6, 14, 25, 39
6:4, 6.................................112
6:12–13.............................169
6:14....................................169
6:18....................................112
6:23......................................92
7:24......................................20
8:1, 5.................................182

8:2......................................107
8:3......................................128
8:3, 4...................................39
8:21....................................154
8:23....................................148
8:29, 38, 39....................107
8:30....................................144
8:33, 38–39.......................20
8:33–34.................................4
8:35ff...................................62
8:37......................................90
9:23....................................106
10:3......................................26
10:5...............................27, 81
10:5, 6, 9...........................30
10:5ff.................................120
11:6......................................71
11:35....................................70
12:1....................................113
14:1, 13............................176
14:14..................................171
14:22–23...........................171
14:23..................................103
15:1–2................................176

1 Corinthians
1:29–31...............................56
1:30.........10, 22, 102, 110
2:16......................................61
3:2......................................179
3:8......................................144
3:10, 11............................102
3:16–17..............................112
4:4..............................45, 140
4:5..47
6:11......................................72
6:19....................................112
7:23....................................181
8:9......................................176
9..84
9:12......................................84

1 Corinthians Continued
9:19, 20, 22 178
10:23-24 178
10:25, 29, 32 176
10:28-29 184
12:12 112
13:2, 13 156
15:19 149

2 Corinthians
1:12 140
4:10 155
4:8-10 107
5:10 143
5:17-21 xx
5:18, 19 80
5:18-19 6
5:19 37
5:19, 21 18
5:21 .... 6, 15, 39
7:1 113
9:6 153
9:7 114

Galatians
1:8-9 xvi
2:3 177
2:3-5 178
2:16 .... xvii, 119
3:6 129
3:8 4
3:10 81
3:10, 12 33
3:11 27
3:11-12 31
3:13 .... 23, 165
3:17 35
3:18 .... 20, 31
3:21, 22 34
4:4 23

4:6 63
4:30 145
5:1, 4 180
5:1-4 166
5:5 122
5:6 35
5:13 177
5:19ff 66
6:9 98
6:17 154

Ephesians
1:3-5 102
1:4 165
1:5-6 6
1:5-7, 13 87
1:6 57
2:4, 5 69
2:6 104
2:8 57
2:8-9 80
2:10 .... 70, 105
2:14 62
2:21 .... 103, 112
3:12 63
3:18-19 90
5:8 112

Philippians
1:6 144
1:29 73
2:12 144
2:13 24
3:8-9 25
3:10-11 .... 107, 155
3:13-14 82
4:11-12 174

Colossians
- 1:4–5 147
- 1:13 104
- 1:14, 20, 21 102
- 1:21 72
- 2:3 22
- 2:9 8
- 3:1 112
- 3:14 156
- 3:24 145

1 Thessalonians
- 3:13 141
- 4:3, 7 .... 112, 165
- 5:9 112

2 Thessalonians
- 1:5–7 154
- 3:13 98

1 Timothy
- 1:5 183
- 1:19 184
- 4:5 172
- 6:17–19 152

2 Timothy
- 1:9 .... 70, 112
- 2:11, 12 107
- 2:20 106
- 3:17 113
- 4:8 150

Titus
- 1:15 173
- 2:11–13 112
- 3:4, 5, 7 70
- 3:7 103

Hebrews
- 2:14 23
- 6:10 154
- 9:14 111
- 10:2 183
- 10:28 152
- 10:29 111
- 11:2 169
- 11:6 .... 28, 69
- 11:13 112
- 13:16 100

James
- 1:12 132
- 2:10 77
- 2:10–11 161
- 2:14 135
- 2:21, 24 133
- 2:21–23 136

1 Peter
- 1:2 73
- 1:5 147
- 1:9 148
- 1:15 112
- 1:18–19 180
- 2:9 58
- 2:11 112
- 3:21 183
- 4:3 106
- 5:5 50

2 Peter
- 1:4 17
- 1:10 107

1 John
- 3:2 17
- 3:3 113
- 3:8, 9 106
- 3:10 112

1 John Continued
    3:24...........................104
    4:10.............................72

4:10, 19....................... 111
4:11............................112
5:12.................... 68, 103

Date Completed	Name

H&E Publishing
www.HesedAndEmet.com

About H&E Publishing

H&E Publishing is a Canadian evangelical publishing company located out of Peterborough, Ontario. We exist to provide Christ-exalting, Gospel-centred, and Bible-saturated content aimed to show God to be as glorious and worthy as He truly is.

We seek to provide rich resources that will equip, nourish, and refresh the Christian's soul. We desire to make available a variety of works that serve this purpose in the church. One key area of focus is to revive evangelicals of the past through updated reprints.

www.ingramcontent.com/pod-product-compliance
Lightning Source LLC
Chambersburg PA
CBHW060521080526
44586CB00012B/565